Language in a Black Community

Multilingual Matters

Books available from College-Hill Press are marked ●.
"Bilingualism: Basic Principles"
HUGO BAETENS BEARDSMORE
"Evaluating Bilingual Education: A Canadian Case Study"
MERRILL SWAIN AND SHARON LAPKIN
"Bilingual Children: Guidance for the Family"
GEORGE SAUNDERS
"Language Attitudes Among Arabic-French Bilinguals in Morocco"
ABDELÂLI BENTAHILA
"Conflict and Language Planning in Quebec"
RICHARD Y. BOURHIS (ed.)
●"Bilingualism and Special Education"
JIM CUMMINS
"Bilingualism or Not: The Education of Minorities"
TOVE SKUTNABB-KANGAS
"An Ethnographic/Sociolinguistic Approach to Language Proficiency Assessment"
CHARLENE RIVERA (ed.)
"Communicative Competence Approaches to Language Proficiency Assessment: Research and Application"
CHARLENE RIVERA (ed.)
"Language Proficiency and Academic Achievement"
CHARLENE RIVERA (ed.)
"Pluralism: Cultural Maintenance and Evolution"
BRIAN BULLIVANT
"Placement Procedures in Bilingual Education: Education and Policy Issues"
CHARLENE RIVERA (ed.)
●"The Education of Linguistic and Cultural Minorities in the OECD Countries"
STACY CHURCHILL
"Learner Language and Language Learning"
CLAUS FAERCH, KIRSTEN HAASTRUP AND ROBERT PHILLIPSON
"Bilingual and Multicultural Education: Canadian Perspectives"
STAN SHAPSON AND VINCENT D'OYLEY (eds.)
"Multiculturalism: The Changing Paradigm"
LOIS FOSTER AND DAVID STOCKLEY
●"Language Acquisition of a Bilingual Child"
ALVINO FANTINI
●"Modelling and Assessing Second Language Acquisition"
KENNETH HYLTENSTAM AND MANFRED PIENEMANN (eds.)
"Aspects of Bilingualism in Wales"
COLIN BAKER
"Minority Education and Ethnic Survival"
MICHAEL BYRAM
"Family Immersion"
MARRIANNE CELCE-MURCIA
●"Age in Second Language Acquisition"
BIRGIT HARLEY
"Pluralism and Schooling in Canada"
JOHN R. MALLEA
●"Language in a Black Community"
VIV EDWARDS

Please contact us for the latest information on recent and forthcoming books in the series.
Derrick Sharp, General Editor, Multilingual Matters,
Bank House, 8a Hill Road, Clevedon, Avon BS21 7HH, England.

Language in a
Black Community

Viv Edwards

COLLEGE-HILL PRESS. San Diego, California

First published by
Multilingual Matters Ltd
Bank House, 8a Hill Road,
Clevedon, Avon BS21 7HH,
England,
as part of a series of books edited by
Derrick Sharp under the heading
Multilingual Matters. Full details of
the other books and related journals are
available from the address above.

British Library Cataloguing in Publication Data

Edwards, Viv
    Language in a black community. — (Multilingual Matters; 24)
    1. English language — Dialects — West Indies
    I. Title
    427'.9729   PE3302

    ISBN 0-905028-53-8
    ISBN 0-905028-52-X Pbk

Library of Congress Cataloging-in-Publication Data

Edwards, Viv.
    Language in a Black community.

    Bibliography: p.
    Includes index.
    1. Blacks—Great Britain—Languages.
    2. Sociolinguistics—Great Britain.   1. Title.
    P40.5.B42E38   1986   401'.9'0896041   85–28037
    ISBN 0-88744-244-7

College-Hill Press Inc.,
4284 41st Street,
San Diego, CA 92105, USA

Copyright © 1986 Viv Edwards

Typeset by Wayside Graphics, Clevedon, Avon.
Printed and bound in Great Britain by
Colourways Press Ltd, Clevedon BS21 6RR.

for Carol Tomlin and Leighton Bruce

Contents

Acknowledgements

The research project on which this book is based was funded by the Economic and Social Research Council, and directed jointly by David Sutcliffe and myself. The present study deals largely with the social and psychological determinants of inter-situational variation in the speech of British born black people. David Sutcliffe's account of intra-situational variation, and, in particular, code-switching behaviour will be published separately by Multilingual Matters. Although the two parts of the project are self-contained and have been written up independently, they are based on the same data. The contribution of David Sutcliffe in the planning of the project and in the fieldwork is gratefully acknowledged.

Warm thanks must also go to the 45 young British Black people from Dudley who took part in the study. Assurances of confidentiality were given these young people and so their names have been changed in the text and they have become numbers in tables and figures. Nonetheless, they remain very real individuals for all those associated with the project, and we are grateful that we had the opportunity to listen to and share their views and experiences.

Carol Tomlin and Leighton Bruce, the fieldworkers on the project, were greatly valued for their resourcefulness, adaptability and good humour. Their ability to communicate their perceptions of the British Black community of which they are a part formed the impetus for the research and sustained it from beginning to end. They and their many friends in Dudley, especially Claudette Rodman and Sandra Pitter, made the period spent on fieldwork a very enjoyable one through their friendship and hospitality.

The team of people who helped in the transcription and coding of the recordings must also be acknowledged. These include Leighton Bruce, Mario da Souza, Adonis Daniel, Carlita Daniel, Jeremy Green, Hilary Fell, Penny Howard, Lindy Kerr, Caroline Lally, Tom Morris, Lindsay Nickels, Sandra Pitter and Carol Tomlin. Two people, however, should be singled out for special thanks — Jeremy Green, who also took part in the actual field-work and was responsible for the technical side of the recording, and Carlita Daniel, who undertook the lion's share of the Patois transcription and coding.

Thanks are due to Lesley Milroy, who acted as consultant for the project, for her encouragement and support from the inception of the project right the way through to its completion, and for her useful and challenging comments on early drafts of the book. I am also very grateful for the help offered by the other people who read and commented on the manuscript, notably Michel Blanc, Jenny Cheshire, Carlita Daniel, Mary Fuller, Paul Meara, David Sutcliffe and Carol Tomlin.

Mary Fuller deserves my very special thanks. The gestation period for the book and her son, James, were almost identical and it sometimes seemed that as much time was spent in detailed discussion of the various versions of the manuscript as on ante-natal care! Her perspective as a sociologist on the subject matter of the book was invaluable.

Last, but by no means least, I would like to thank my husband Chris Morriss and to my children Dafydd, Ceri and Siân for their patience and forebearance, and my parents, Tom and Hett Edwards for their continuing love and support.

1 Introduction

This book is the first of two reports on a research project on British Black language, based on fieldwork undertaken in Dudley, West Midlands in the summer of 1982.[1] It is essentially a sociolinguistic study which aims to identify the range of language which we found in this community and its social and situational determinants. There are many questions which relate to research design, methodology and analysis which are of primary interest to linguists. However, the fact that the study is based on a British Black community means that its findings are of interest to a much broader audience which includes teachers, sociologists, speech therapists, youth and community workers and, of course, black people themselves.

The interface of varieties of British English and Caribbean Creoles is a new and exciting development. The wide range of linguistic behaviour which exists within the British Black community poses many challenges for description. It also raises questions of theoretical importance for language acquisition and language change. Interest in this area to date has been limited to a small number of researchers, and it is only very recently that British linguists have begun to awaken to the enormous potential for study opened up by the contact between these different speech communities.

Black language patterns are also of considerable interest to teachers who form the section of white mainstream society which often has the most direct and sustained contact with black children. Teacher interest in this area has always been high, and many of the attempts to understand black language have either been undertaken or initiated by teachers. Sometimes teachers asked questions which would never have occurred to linguists; on other occasions they sought information which linguists were not in a position to provide. As a result, many teacher assumptions based on inaccurate or incomplete information have become a part of conventional wisdom, and sometimes inform teacher practice with unfortunate results. Any study which deals with empirical evidence on the nature of black language will thus be relevant to teachers who wish to understand the linguistic background of the children they are working with.

Speech therapists are another group of people who need accurate information. Interest in this area has been slow and most of the theory and practice in language pathology is based on work with monolingual subjects in monolingual societies (see, however, Cummins, 1984; Miller, 1984). For the successful diagnosis and treatment of speech defects in the British Black and other non-standard English speaking communities, a full picture of the linguistic norms which are associated with these populations is essential.

An appreciation of black language behaviour is also of importance for harmonious race relations. Although it would seem that most young black people speak a variety of English very close to, or indistinguishable from, the local white norm in their interaction with white people, some individuals show evidence of markedly black speech even in very formal encounters with people such as teachers and the police. It is important to understand the symbolic meaning of behaviour of this kind and the reasons which underlie it. To dismiss such language as "strange" or "exaggerated" is to fail to grasp the realities of life in white Britain for black people, and the limited courses of action which many black youths feel are open to them. It also underestimates the extent of linguistic diversity and the importance of black culture within the British Black community.

Last, but by no means least, many black people will share an interest in attempts to describe the range of language behaviour which is to be found in the British Black community. The aim of the present study is to attempt to formalize certain areas of the native speaker's intuition, and to make these insights accessible to those outside the community. It is also hoped that the findings which emerge will strongly challenge some of the negative stereotypes about black language which are to be found both in mainstream white society and in the black community.

Black language and linguists

Varieties of Black English in Britain constitute an exciting, but underexplored, area of study. Despite a considerable body of opinion that research in this area is an important priority (e.g. Bullock, 1975; Little & Willey, 1981; Rampton, 1981), progress has been depressingly slow. Britain lags behind the USA in this respect. During the late 1960s, concern in educational circles about the underachievement of black children gave a boost to the development of sociolinguistics. This, in turn, led to important descriptions of black varieties of American English (cf. Shuy, Wolfram & Riley, 1968; Labov *et al.*, 1968) and extensive discussion of the implications of dialect difference for education (e.g. Labov, 1969; 1972; 1982). For the first time non-standard dialects of English were recognized as a legitimate object of linguistic study.

This work proved highly influential in many parts of the world. In the West Indies, for instance, the contact between the various West African languages spoken by slaves and the European languages of the planters led to the development, in the first instance, of simple pidgins and, later, to autonomous languages or creoles. Like non-standard dialects, creole-speaking situations are characterized by considerable linguistic variation. For many writers, this posed a serious challenge to the notion of the homogeneous speech community posited by Chomsky (1965), which had become a part of linguistic orthodoxy. Creole studies developed at a very rapid rate, particularly in the Caribbean (cf. Hymes, 1971), from a fringe interest to an area of central concern for linguistic theory.

It is only very recently that attention has been paid to the languages of the many different peoples who have come to Britain in the post-war period (Trudgill, 1984; Linguistic Minorities Project, 1984). Indigenous Celtic languages have fared a little better and have received attention from both social psychologists (e.g. Bourhis & Giles, 1976; Giles, 1971) and sociologists of language (e.g. Dorian, 1981; Mackinnon, 1977). But growth of sociolinguistics in Britain has been mainly in the direction of indigenous non-standard dialects of English (cf. Trudgill, 1974; Trudgill, 1978; Milroy, 1980; Cheshire, 1982). West Indian language has given rise to considerably less interest. The main accounts to date (V. Edwards, 1979, 1983; Sutcliffe, 1982a) rely heavily on Caribbean descriptions, and our understanding of linguistic and social constraints which operate on the speech of young British born blacks is sadly incomplete.

Black language and teachers

The main call for a study of non-indigenous language has come in Britain, as it did in America, not from linguists but from teachers, and a great deal of the discussion of this area has been framed in terms of the educational implications of linguistic diversity (cf. V. Edwards, 1979, 1983; Richmond, 1979). The situation concerning non-English speaking immigrants was summed up in fairly simplistic terms. The overall aim, at least in the 1960s and 1970s, was assimilation and the acquisition of English was an essential step in this process. It was only in the mid-1970s when the children of New Commonwealth immigrants reached adolescence and sometimes would not, or could not, communicate with their parents in their first language that the importance of mother tongue teaching became first a community and later an educational issue (cf. V. Edwards, 1983).

Attitudes towards the children of West Indian immigrants have always been more confused. The prevailing attitude was that they spoke English, but that it was a "broken" variety. There was a total absence of policy for the teaching of English to West Indian children. It was not felt appropriate to use the techniques employed with non-English speaking children, yet it was recognized that West Indian children could not compete on a par with their white peers until they acquired British English. One solution was to place children in remedial streams, irrespective of their actual abilities; another, possibly more common, response was total inertia (cf. Townsend, 1971).

The absence of a central policy in the case of both non-English speaking and West Indian children had quite considerable educational consequences. Different Local Education Authorities and different schools within each authority developed different strategies and there was little pooling of ideas or resources (V. Edwards, 1984). Nonetheless, there seemed to be a more coherent view of the nature and extent of the problems of non-English speaking children.

The confusion surrounding the language of West Indian children can be illustrated, for instance, by looking at the funding of the first major projects to develop teaching materials for ethnic minority children. Immigration from the Caribbean started a little earlier than from the rest of the New Commonwealth, and West Indian immigrants were no less numerous than non-English speaking immigrants. Nonetheless, the Schools Council Project for the Teaching of English to Immigrant Pupils received a budget twice as large as Concept 7–9, the sister project for West Indian children, and published its materials some five years earlier. Although Concept 7–9 was originally designed for West Indian children, only one section of the materials addressed the question of dialect; the rest was concerned with concepts and verbal strategies which it was felt would be helpful for a wide range of children, and not only West Indians.

The early 1970s marked the realization that West Indian children were seriously underachieving in school (e.g. Coard, 1971; Townsend, 1971). The first official recognition that language might be playing a role in this process came with the publication of the Select Committee on Race Relations and Immigration report on Education in 1973. It advocated more attention to the teaching of English and suggested that while language was by no means the only reason for the underperformance of West Indian children it was one which was now acknowledged and could be "dealt with".

It was never made clear what precise steps should be taken to "deal with" this question. During this period, the only easily available information for teachers on the language of West Indian children was Concept 7–9 and a small number of related publications (e.g. Wight & Norris, 1970; Wight, 1971), and some short pamphlets distributed by the Community Relations Commission. The more diligent could seek out specialist Caribbean publications like *Jamaican Creole Syntax* (Bailey, 1966) and the *Dictionary of Jamaican English* (Cassidy & Le Page, 1967), or the more popularized account, *Jamaica Talk* (Cassidy, 1961). On educational issues, guidance could be sought only from American work in this area and publications like *Teaching Black Children to Read* (Baratz & Shuy, 1969) proved influential in some teacher circles.

Caribbean critics (Craig, 1981; D'Costa, 1981) lament the fact that teachers and linguists have overlooked the great progress which has been made in the West Indies in the area of language in education. There have been important developments in syllabus design (Carrington & Borley, 1977) and teaching materials (Wilson, Craig & Campbell, 1979), and a number of very useful discussions of the main issues are now widely available (see, for instance, Craig, 1976, and Wilson, 1978). There is no doubt that, had the studies put out by the Language Materials Workshop of the University of the West Indies been available in the early days of immigration, they would have been invaluable. By the mid 1970s, however, the British situation had undergone some very important changes. The legislation enacted through the 1960s meant that immigration had come to a virtual halt by the end of the decade. Almost all children entering schools by the mid 1970s had been born in Britain, and most were able to speak a variety of English indistinguishable from, or very close to, the local white norm.

Even if the Caribbean materials had been developed by this point, the case for using them would have been difficult to argue. Black children were showing a wide range of linguistic behaviour and no criteria existed for deciding who could benefit from structured teaching of the kind recommended by Caribbean writers. In my experience it was often the children with behaviour problems rather than language differences who were singled out by class teachers for specialist help. Classroom dynamics would also have needed to be taken into account, including the reactions of non-black children and black children whom the teacher considered did not need specialist intervention. Equally important, any attempt on the part of a white teacher to teach standard English might have been interpreted as yet another act of oppression in a climate where identifiably black speech was emerging as a symbol of group identity.

Black language and speech therapists

In America in the 1960s it was not uncommon for Black English to be considered deviant, and many perfectly normal black children were singled out as suitable candidates for speech therapy. One writer even coined the term "dialectolalia" to describe this condition (see, Baratz, 1968 for a discussion of this area). However, the realization during the late 1960s and early 1970s that non-standard dialects of English were merely different from the standard rather than in some way deficient has informed practice in the area of language disability in both America and Britain.

There is no documentation concerning the reactions of speech therapists to the language of newly arrived West Indian children. However, my own experience of talking with people who work in this area suggests that there was considerable confusion as to what constituted "normal" and "abnormal" language use. Because black children often did not mark plurals, possessives and third person singular present tense verbs with *s* ("boy" for "boys"; "John book" for "John's book"; "he go" for "he goes"), it was sometimes assumed they could not pronounce this sound. I have heard reports, even relatively recently, of black children being referred to speech therapists for remediation in this area, even though there is nothing linguistically deviant about this behaviour.

The problems facing speech therapists and teachers of language disordered children have in no way been diminished by the fact that today many young black people speak like their white peers. The tasks of diagnosis and remediation will remain extremely difficult until descriptions of the range of language norms to be found in the British Black community become available. Unless the practitioner is aware of the different varieties to which children are exposed, it is impossible to decide firstly *whether* the child's speech is deviant, and, secondly, the *extent* to which a child's speech is deviant or reflecting the norms of another speech community.

Black language and race relations

White observers of black language risk forming quite inaccurate conclusions about what is taking place. There is a tendency to assume, for instance, that, because black youths speak with a Birmingham or a Cockney accent, Caribbean language is no longer an important social force in their lives. Alternatively, white people assume that there is a simple dichotomy in which black people speak Caribbean varieties at home and English elsewhere. Such a position is disturbingly unimaginative. As we will see, all or almost all young black people use markedly black speech in certain situations. These situations vary from person to person, as does the amount of distinctively black speech. Variation depends on a wide range of extra-linguistic factors, including sensitivity to situation and topic. The suggestion that most British Black people do not speak Patois overlooks the considerable diversity which exists and the symbolic functions fulfilled by the various aspects of young people's linguistic repertoires.

There is also a tendency for white observers to recoil from young black people who choose to use distinctively black speech, either to one another or when interacting with white people. In some cases, whites perceive that they are — very effectively — being excluded from the conversation and feel unsure as to how they should react. On other occasions they feel threatened and think that the young people concerned are simply taking things too far. An understanding of *why* some British blacks choose to behave in this way is fundamental for good race relations. Any white person who simply dismisses these choices without further thought is seriously underestimating the complexities of life in a predominantly white society for black people, and is likely to exacerbate the situation still further.

Black language and black people[2]

West Indian Creoles have a relatively recent literary history and, although a growing amount of poetry and other writing by British Black authors is beginning to appear (e.g. L. K. Johnson, 1981; J. Johnson, 1978), black language is associated in most people's minds with oral culture. It is unfortunately true that languages which are the vehicles of a written literature are considered more prestigious than those which are not. In a British context, Geordie or Cockney, for instance, is not held in the same esteem as standard English. And it is only in relatively recent years that linguists have come to realize that spoken languages — with or without written literature — are legitimate objects of study in their own right. The tremendous growth of popular accounts of British dialects (see Edwards, Trudgill & Weltens, 1984), however, can leave little doubt as to the extent of non-specialist interest in this area. The fact that *Jamaica Talk* (Cassidy, 1961) is now in its third edition, suggests a similar level of interest in Caribbean language.

The project on which the present book is based was undertaken by white linguists and thus risks arousing understandable suspicions in black readers. The long history of racist attitudes towards black language has manifested itself either in the neglect of study, or in the promotion of "pathological" arguments. Herskovits (1937), for instance, reports that until the late 1930s, the most common hypothesis put forward to explain Black American speech was that it was "the blind groping of minds too primitive in modes of speech beyond their capabilities". More recently, the same pathological framework is to be detected in the work of researchers who chose to talk in terms of "language deprivation" (Wight, 1971; Whiteman, Brown & Deutsch, 1967).

The present account attempts to tap some of the richness and complexity of language use in the British Black community, and totally rejects the view that black language is in any way inadequate or inferior. It has been undertaken by white researchers because, at the time the project was conceived, no black linguists were working in the area of British Black language. Although I am very conscious of possible accusations of linguistic colonialism, the failure to document new and exciting developments of Caribbean language in a British setting seems a far more serious charge.

Native speaker status guarantees neither objectivity nor a monopoly of insight. However, it must be admitted that there are many disadvantages in studying another language from the position of an "outsider". It is very easy to interpret both the form and function of British Black language through a white cultural and linguistic matrix. In order to guard as far as possible against this bias, I have attempted at all times to cross-check my own impressions, and to draw on the intuitions of the black fieldworkers and many other black people associated in various ways with the project.

I hope that the description which results is an accurate reflection of these intuitions. If the conclusions from the study break no new ground for the British Black reader, I will indeed have achieved this aim, for it should be remembered that these conclusions are by no means obvious to "outsiders". I hope that I have faithfully captured and communicated some of the complexity and subtlety of British Black language for those who view it from outside.

The present study

The present study is an attempt to look at the current linguistic situation of British born black children. It focuses on the speech and opinions of young people from Dudley in the West Midlands in order to ask — and, hopefully, to answer — a range of questions which have previously been matters of speculation. Many current opinions are based on discussions with young black people in racially mixed situations, such as school. It is generally held, for instance, that the language of British born blacks is indistinguishable from that of their white peers, and that "Patois" — the most common community term for Caribbean language varieties — is used regularly only by a very small proportion of British born blacks (cf. Rosen & Burgess, 1980). Such opinions, however, are based on the reports of children to white teacher researchers and fail to take into account that the low status of black language in mainstream white society may have led to under-reporting. In the absence of authentic speech data or an intimate understanding of the black community, it is impossible to predict just how these young people will behave in black peer group conversation.

Frequent reference is also made to the fact that many British Blacks who show no signs of Patois usage in their early years take pride in "talking black" by the time they are 14 or 15 years of age, as a conscious act of identity. The young people who take this course are generally held to be those who have chosen a life style associated with "black youth culture", which revolves around reggae, Rastafarianism and other specifically black forms of culture (cf. Crump, 1979). There is noticeable absence of discussion about the role which Patois may play in the lives of other young Black people, such as the substantial minority of Pentecostal Christians. We are left to conclude that Patois is of symbolic significance only to those Black Britons who choose to use it in their interactions with whites.

Any attempt to represent linguistic reality needs to improve on the greatest part of existing research in two important and fundamental ways. First, conclusions must be based on an actual corpus of data rather than self-reports. Second, methodology must be improved so as to ensure that this corpus authentically reflects the range of individual and situational variation which exists within the black community.

Writing for a mixed audience: The organization of the book

A book which addresses the question of language in a British Black community is likely to draw on a wide audience. In addition to linguists in general and sociolinguists in particular, sociologists and educators, and social and youth workers whose work touches in various ways upon the lives of the British Black community, will appreciate the importance of language for young black people. It is therefore important to present the findings of the present study in a way which is accessible to non-linguists without in any way oversimplifying the issues involved.

The book falls into two main parts. The first part sets the scene for the study. Chapter 2 describes the social, economic and political realities of life in Britain for black people. Its aim is to outline the diversity of the black community and the many different ways in which individuals have responded to the realities of racial inequality. Such an understanding is essential if we are to be able to isolate the likely social constraints on linguistic behaviour. Chapter 3 summarizes the work which has been done to date on black language in Britain. It examines the shortcomings of our present knowledge of this area, and outlines the most pressing questions which need attention. Chapter 4 describes the sociolinguistic framework for analysis and examines some of the theoretical assumptions which underpin the present study. It is therefore of more specific interest to linguists than to other readers. Chapter 5 describes the isolation of social variables and the composition of the

sample. Chapter 6 considers the issues for the fieldworker in data collection. These chapters are also of a more specialist nature, but should
nonetheless be well within the grasp of readers without a knowledge of
linguistics.

The second part of the book reports the findings of the project.
Chapter 7 provides a quantitative analysis of the data and examines the
relations between frequency of Patois usage and a wide range of social
correlates, including formality, ethnicity, network relations, sex, education and attitudes towards mainstream white society. Chapter 8 considers
whether some young people are more competent Patois speakers than
others and whether differing degrees of competence are in any way determined by social factors. Chapter 9 attempts to answer the question: "What
constitutes Patois usage?" It examines different patterns of Patois usage
and their social correlates and discusses the symbolic functions of Patois
usage. Finally Chapter 10 presents the conclusions which emerge from the
study and considers promising directions for future research.

In order to make the text more accessible to non-specialists, full descriptions of linguistic variables are contained in the Appendices; so, too, is
specific information on the statistical procedures employed in the study and
more detailed discussion of the results.

A note on terminology

It is common in linguistics for a researcher to refer to "informants",
and in both linguistics and the social sciences, to talk of "subjects".
Terminology of this kind is used in a neutral and non-evaluative way by
specialists, but can give rise to serious misunderstanding when encountered by readers who approach the subject from a different perspective.
For this reason, a deliberate decision has been made to use "participants" or "speakers" and it is hoped that this choice of expression
reflects to some extent the respect which the present researchers feel for
those who took part in the study. It has also been decided, for the same
reason, to use the community term "Patois" rather than the linguists'
formulation "Creole".

Choice of terminology does not, of course, guarantee freedom of bias.
It is in the very nature of the task that we are unlikely to have avoided all the
pitfalls. It is hoped, however, that the worst excesses of even the best
motivated linguists have been overcome. We have certainly avoided the
unintentional colonial bias of one researcher who felt moved to write in
terms of "*my* speakers"!

Notes to Chapter 1

1. The second report, *Language Symbolism*, is being prepared by David Sutcliffe and will be published by Multilingual Matters.
2. "Black" is used by some writers to refer to all non-white people in Britain. However, in the present context and throughout this book, it is used for Afro-Caribbean Settlers and their British-born children and grandchildren.

2 Black people in Britain

Although Black people have formed a part of the fabric of British life since Elizabethan times (cf. Walvin, 1982), their presence was restricted until the 1950s to a relatively few locations and the actual numbers involved were very small. The post-war period, however, was marked by a rapid migration of British citizens from the New Commonwealth who came in response to much discussed "pull and push" factors (cf. Peach, 1969). On the one hand, they were driven to seek work abroad by chronic unemployment or pressure on the land. On the other hand, they were drawn to Britain by the serious labour shortages. The boom economy was creating many thousands of new jobs. British workers were taking advantage of opportunities for upward mobility, one of the consequences of which was an obstinate residue of vacancies in the transport sector, the National Health service and other industries which had a history of low pay and anti-social work hours.

The traditional destination for West Indians had been America, but new legislation enacted there in the early 1950s restricted their entry. The United Kingdom thus became the obvious focus for migration. Job opportunities and ease of access were the most important of the factors which attracted immigrants, but there were also strong links between the West Indies and Britain. Government and education had been modelled on the British system; school curricula were dominated by British history and English literature to the exclusion of all things Caribbean. There was thus a feeling of home-coming for most West Indians arriving in England. Hiro (1973) graphically captures this feeling when he describes Britain as the "historico-cultural navel" and migration as "a journey to the cultural womb".

At first the rate of immigration was very rapid. Between 1955 and 1961 official statistics show that some 200,000 people had arrived in Britain. The 1960s saw the enactment of increasingly more stringent immigration control. Although there are indications that this flow had begun to slow down, the prospect of restricted entry to the country in the near future had the effect of accelerating the rate of migration, particularly towards the end of the decade. The West Indian population of Britain in 1971 was estimated at 543,000, just over 1% of the population. Since this time the very limited number of new immigrants arriving in Britain has in fact been smaller than that of those returning to the West Indies, and this situation is likely to have remained unchanged.

Frustrated hopes

The reality of life in Britain was dramatically different from the vision which most migrants had nurtured. On a human level, the anger and frustration experienced by West Indians confronted with the indifference and hostility of the white population has been sensitively captured in novels like Selvon's *The Lonely Londoners* and Salkey's *The Adventures of Catullus Kelly*. The material realities have been encapsulated in a whole series of reports, but most notably the three surveys published by The Policy Studies Institute (PSI) (Daniel, 1968; Smith, 1976; Brown, 1984). The mismatch between expectations and reality can be clearly illustrated by examining the progress of black people over the last 20 or so years in two critical areas, employment and education.

Employment

PSI reports have shown consistently that black workers are concentrated in unskilled and semi-skilled work that there are substantial differences between median weekly wages of indigenous and immigrants groups; and that promotion opportunities are far more limited for black workers. Whereas unemployment was not an issue in the sixties, it has become the focus for increasing concern throughout the seventies, particularly in the black community where a disproportionately high number of adults cannot find work. The most recent estimate (Brown, 1984) suggests that one-and-a-half times as many blacks as whites are registered as unemployed. This trend is particularly marked for males over the age of 35 who live outside Inner London, Birmingham and Manchester, for whom the rates of unemployment are between twice and three times higher than for the white population. There are also substantial differences in the average length of unemployment for West Indian and white workers so that, for instance, the proportion of black people who have been registered as unemployed for a year or more is three times higher. It should also be remembered that an estimated 5% of black youths under the age of 25 do not consider registration as unemployed a realistic step in finding work and are therefore not included in official statistics.

It is important to appreciate that the current employment prospects of black people in Britain are a continuation of an uninterrupted pattern of inequality. The formal recognition of this inequality is embodied in documents such as the most recent PSI survey (Brown, 1984) which concludes that

> "Examination of the changes in the employment patterns of white, Asian and West Indian people over the eight years between 1974 and 1982 shows that there has been little convergence of the types of work done by the majority and minority ethnic groups, while their unemployment rates have sharply diverged." (p. 293)

The same facts are articulated somewhat less dispassionately by the new generation of young black poets and writers. *Inglan is a Bitch*, a poem by Lindon Kwesi Johnson, for instance, charts the working life of a black man on the underground, dishwashing, digging ditches and finally working in a factory. It finishes —

> *well mi dhu day wok an mi dhu night wok*
> *mi dhu clean wok an' mi dhu dutty wok*
> *dem seh dat black man is very lazy*
> *but if y'u si how mi wok y'u woulda sey mi crazy*
>
> *Inglan is a bitch*
> *dere's no escapin' it*
> *Inglan is a bitch*
> *y'u better face up to it*
>
> *dem have a likkle facktri up inna Brackly*
> *inna disya facktri all dem dhu is pack crackry*
> *fi di laas fifteen years dem get mi laybah*
> *now awftah fifteen years me fall out a fayvah*
>
> *Inglan is a bitch*
> *dere's no escapin' it*
> *Inglan is a bitch*
> *dere's no runnin' whey fram it*
>
> *mi know dem have work, work in abundant*
> *yet still, dem make mi redundant*
> *now, at fifty-five mi gettin' quite ol'*
> *yet still, dem sen' me fi goh draw dole*
>
> *Inglan is a bitch*
> *dere's no escapin' it*
> *Inglan is a bitch fi true*
> *is whey wi a goh dhu 'bout it?*

Education

The position of black children in education is scarcely less depressing. Although parental aspirations and support for children have always been high (cf. Bagley, Bart & Wong, 1979; Tomlinson, 1984), the ability or willingness of British schools and teachers to help West Indian children to fulfil their potential has been seriously questioned. Schools in the inner city areas where immigrants settled were already poorly resourced and under pressure in the 1950s and 1960s (cf. Plowden, 1967), and were not at all equipped to respond effectively to large numbers of new children arriving throughout the school year. There was confusion as to the nature of their language needs, since parents insisted that their children speak "English", but both children and teachers experienced considerable communication difficulties, at least in the early years of migration. There was a disturbing lack of guidance from central government and actual practice was informed more by expediency than by thoughtful and informed policy making (cf. V. Edwards, 1984). Very often the solution was to place children in low streams and remedial classes, irrespective of their actual ability.

This pattern produced a national picture, first officially recognized in the Statistics of Education (DES, 1970), in which disproportionately low numbers of black children were to be found in selective schools, higher streams and examination classes. They were also seriously over-represented in schools for the educationally sub-normal. The placement of black children in ESN schools became a highly emotional issue in the early seventies. As the extent of wrongful placement became more widely known (publicized, for instance, by the highly influential pamphlet by Coard, *How the West Indian Child is Made Educationally Sub-Normal in the British School System*), the ESN issue became the rallying point for much broader anxiety and disquiet with the educational performance of black children.

The DES abandoned racial classification in the collection of educational statistics in 1973. Dissatisfaction had been expressed about the definition of "immigrant" which was based on parents' length of stay in Britain and was unrelated to actual educational need (cf. V. Edwards, 1983). More recently, however, some teacher and community organizations have argued that statistics which make use of racial classifications would allow more effective monitoring of ethnic minority children's academic progress and be extremely valuable in informing educational policy (cf. Rampton, 1981). For the present it is difficult to construct an accurate picture of what is taking place, though there are strong indications that there has been little convergence between the levels of achievement of white and black children. The 1980 ILEA Literacy Survey (Mabey, 1981), for instance, showed that the mean reading levels of West Indian pupils at 8, 10 and 15 years were significantly lower than those of children born to non-immigrant parents. Rampton (1981) suggests that the gap between West Indian and other children is still apparent and that this gap widens as children make their way through school. However, there are indications that West Indian girls perform better than boys (Driver, 1980; Fuller, 1983).

The most usual explanation put forward for the underperformance of West Indian children in the early days of migration was that they were experiencing "temporary problems" of adjustment and language. Later, it was argued that one of the consequences for black children of living in a racist society is a lowered self-esteem, and early formulations of "multicultural education" were based on the assumption that children would view themselves more positively and perform better academically if the school acknowledged and respected minority languages and cultures. The notion of negative self-concept has been strongly challenged both in the black community and in the research literature (see, for example, Stone, 1981; Milner, 1983) and there has been a corresponding shift in the discussion of this area from "multicultural education" to "anti-racist teaching".

There has thus been a significant shift from a largely pathological stance, which attributes blame for underperformance to features intrinsic to the minority community, to a view which takes into account structural forces in the host society. Rampton (1981), for instance, makes a significant departure from previous official reports by arguing that, although very few teachers are overtly racist, unintentional racism in schools has an important effect on the level of educational achievement of black children. The report is particularly critical of in-service and initial teacher training and draws attention to the stereotyped views and lowered expectations of black pupils which are prevalent among teachers.

Responses to inequality

Much has been written about the response of black people to the systematic inequalities which confront them as a group. This is an area which is beset with difficulties. There are sufficient shared aspects of culture and experience to make it reasonable to talk in terms of "the British Black community". However, there are also important differences which must be fully understood if the observer is to avoid making dangerous and inaccurate overgeneralizations. These differences include whether black persons have been born in Britain, or whether they came originally from the West Indies. The age at which they came can also be a critical factor, since the expectations of someone who migrated as an adult may well be very different from those who were still children when they left the West Indies. Equally important individual differences in personality and experience are likely to exert considerable influence on responses to life in Britain.

Black youth culture

Frequent reference is made in the literature to black youth culture, though this term is seldom rigorously defined. It is particularly prevalent in discussions of the education of young black people where its general characteristics would seem to be disaffection with mainstream white society and adherence to an all-black life-style. The reggae music and lyrics which proclaim the oppression of black people (cf. L. Johnson, 1976) form an important focus for black youth culture, and are an essential feature of many black activities and meeting places such as specialist record shops, parties, sound systems (mobile discotheques) and youth clubs. There is a danger, however, that "black youth culture" will be interpreted as a monolithic structure, whereas in fact it encompasses a very wide range of attitudes and life-styles. It is therefore open to the criticism that it devalues the considerable diversity and individuality which is to be found in British Black and any other societies, and its usefulness as a descriptive or analytical tool is questionable.

Other writers have attempted much finer categorizations. Wood (1974), for instance, talks in terms of mainstreamers, saints, swingers, teenyboppers and black power. Pryce (1979) postulates six different groups: hustlers, teenyboppers, proletarian respectables, saints, mainliners and in-betweeners. Troyna (1979) discusses black youths in Britain in terms of mainstreamers, compromisers and rejectors. Henry, Joshua & Sargeant (1982) outline a typology of Afro-Caribbean identities which includes West Indians, colonial settlers, civil rights blacks, black nationalists and Pan-Africanists. Whereas "black youth culture" has the unfortunate effect of lumping together individuals who often vary from one another in important ways, other schemes of analysis may have equally unfortunate effects. Sometimes they accord group status to the relatively small numbers on the criminal fringe and risk confirming widely held negative stereotypes of black people (Figueroa, 1982). Sometimes they create categories which have little subjective or objective reality for the community which is being studied. These labels have been offered by the analyst and can be usefully contrasted with two named subgroups within the black community — Rastafarians and Christians — which are recognized and defined by black people themselves.

Rastafarianism

The Rastafarian movement started in Jamaica in the 1930s, building on the concepts and categories first expounded by Marcus Garvey. Ras Tafari, the personal name of Haile Sellassie I of Ethiopia, was proclaimed as the living God who would use his power to help all black people to return to Africa. Sellasie's failure to intervene ultimately created what some observers (cf. Cashmore, 1979) have termed an "ideological vacuum" and there was a gradual shift of focus from the return to Africa to liberation in Jamaica.

Rastafarianism, like other millenial movements, was born out of the despair of an oppressed people who sought to remodel the basic elements of their social order. The white colonial system in Jamaica was identified as the seat of all evil and black people's redemption lay in refusing to accept the inferior status doled out to them by white people. By fully recognizing their own worth, Rastafarians are able to approach life's problems as equal members of the human race. The two fold nature of this humanity — our individuality and our common condition — are encapsulated in the Rastafarian expression "I-an-I". The emphasis of Rastafarian belief is thus on cultural independence and not on racial separation.

An important feature of Rastafarianism was the creation of certain quite distinct physical traits which marked them out as a group. The most obvious of these traits was the growth of dreadlocks — hair twisted into coils and left to grow naturally in emulation of Ethiopian warriors. Men wear tams, usually in red, gold and green, the colours of the Ethiopian flag; women wear headscarves or turbans. Cashmore (1979: 160) describes these developments as "symbolic responses to the perception and feeling of powerlessness and cultural anonymity".

It is not difficult to understand the appeal of Rastafarianism for young British Blacks, particularly those who had left the Caribbean as children, and were experiencing the gulf between community expectations and the reality of life in Britain. When their parents had set out from Jamaica, Rastafarianism was a rather disreputable cult, for it was not until the late 1960s and 1970s that the movement gained greater credibility and the acquiescence of political figures like Michael Manley (cf. Cashmore, 1979). The main source of information about the concepts of Rastafarianism was reggae music, the musical vehicle of the movement, which gained in popularity throughout the 1970s, and not their parents (cf. L. Johnson, 1976; Garrison, 1979).

Black Pentecostalism

Black Pentecostalism is illustrative of a quite different response to the realities of life in Britain. A very high proportion of West Indian migrants were regular Church goers. Their experience in England, however, was of a highly secularized society in which even those corners of practising Christianity were often cold and unwelcoming. Sutcliffe & Tomlin (in press), for instance, report anecdotal accounts of sandwiches handed around after the service, but not offered to the new member. The style of worship also posed some difficulties. The Pentecostal tradition from which most West Indians came was emotional and participative and thus contrasted sharply with the more formal and reserved services which characterized most British churches.

The basic tenet of Pentecostal doctrine is that all believers are open to an influx of the spirit as in the first Day of the Pentecost. Members or "saints" should live a life as free as possible from the contamination of the outside world in expectation of the Day of Judgement. A very firm commitment is demanded from members in the form of regular attendance at two Sunday services and other activities, such as Bible Class or choir practice, during the week. There is a very strong moral code which prescribes the form of dress, sexual conduct and other aspects of behaviour.

West Indians in Britain, dissatisfied both with their reception in Britain and the forms of worship available to them, began to gather round a particular Pastor, usually meeting in each other's homes. As congregations grew they moved first into halls and later acquired or built permanent Church premises. It is estimated that there are currently 650 black Pentecostal Churches, with 40,000 members and perhaps between two and three times that number of regular worshippers. Black churches are not simply the stronghold of first generation West Indians. They continue to attract young British-born people, though the number of females greatly outnumbers that of males. Sutcliffe & Tomlin (in press) profile male worshippers as the Pastor, one or two young aspiring Pastors; men over the age of 40, though in smaller numbers than women of their age; young musicians who accompany the service; and very few others.

The speech events (preaching, testimony and prayer) which characterize Pentecostalism fit extremely well into an Afro-Caribbean cultural matrix. Sutcliffe & Tomlin point to the patterns of call and response, proverbial expression, exaggerated language, image making and metaphor and tonal sound effects which have all been attested as part of the Afro-Caribbean culture generally (cf. Kochman, 1972; Smitherman, 1981). The form of worship practised by many blacks in America, Jamaica and later in Britain thus represents a remodelling of Christianity within an essentially African framework.

Some observers (for example, Cashmore, 1979) have described the growth of Pentecostalism as "evasion" —

"By attempting to develop their own autonomous religions and find satisfaction within them rather than in the fierce outside world,

the blacks de-emphasised their presence and passively withdrew
into their racially distinct enclaves where they could find mutual
support and encouragement from fellow blacks." (p.41)

Others (e.g. Marks, 1982) argue that the Church is actually a basis for
radicalism. In spite of the conservative nature of their worship, Pentecostal
Christians have been responsible for the organization of an impressive
programme of self-help which includes remedial teaching, vocational training, legal counselling, family casework and the financing of home buying.
Social initiatives on this scale clearly reach well beyond Church membership
into the black community as a whole. Hill (quoted in Marks, 1982) summarizes these developments thus:

> "I've noticed a significant change in the social attitudes of the black
> Pentecostal churches in Britain since about 1975. From what we
> call a 'world-denying ethos' they have moved over to a 'world-
> affirming ethos', functioning in a white society at a social level, and
> within the past couple of years beginning to play a political role. If
> this momentum is maintained they will become a very powerful
> social group. What we are seeing is the emergence of the most
> significant section of the Caribbean community in Britain. The
> black Pentecostal churches command the support of about 20 per
> cent of the community. There is no other group of that size."

West Indian or British Black?

The most obvious effect of immigration legislation is the creation of
distinctively British Black as opposed to West Indian communities in
Britain. The first children of post war immigrants were born in Britain in the
late 1950s. Throughout the 1960s the proportion of British as opposed to
Caribbean born children gradually increased. Most importantly, since 1970
virtually all children of West Indian immigrants have been born in the
United Kingdom. The experience of an entire generation who have been
born or have spent most of their lives in Britain is clearly very different from
their Caribbean born and educated parents. "British Black" is a far more
accurate description of the young people in the present study than "West
Indian".

First generation West Indian immigrants are stereotypically portrayed
as acquiescent, stoical and uncomplaining. Such a view, however, is based
on popular stereotypes rather than research evidence (cf. Allen, 1982) and
there were undoubtedly many individuals who, from the earliest days of
migration, openly questioned the justice of the treatment of black people. It
would also be inaccurate to suggest a complete discontinuity between British

children and their West Indian born parents. Both generations share many common values and cultural experiences. For example, a significant minority of young British Black people attend Church and conform closely to parental expectations of how they should behave.

Nonetheless, British born black people lead a life which is qualitatively very different from that of their parents. They have received a British education, and have mainly been exposed to the British media. Their experience of the police is also likely to be different. Black people of all ages complain of harrassment by the police, but young males are particularly likely to be stopped (cf. Scarman, 1981). Many of the young people who took part in the present study had been stopped and questioned repeatedly by the police for offences which they had not committed, and all had a close friend or relative who had undergone this treatment. Whereas the anger and frustration of West Indian immigrants went largely unnoticed by mainstream white society, there can be no doubt as to the hostility of their British-born children to the realities of racial inequality.

Social diversity and linguistic diversity

Ethnic groups are in no way homogeneous wholes. The picture which emerges of "the British Black community" is one of a people who are united by the experience of being black in Britain with all its social and economic concomitants, but differentiated by a wide range of attitudes and responses to this experience. Some groups, like the Rastafarians, demand cultural independence from mainstream white society, and refuse to accept the inferior status associatd with black people. Other groups, like the Pentecostal Christians, have tended, until recently at least, to take a more indirect course, avoiding confrontation with the mainstream society. Some individuals attempt to assimilate to the dominant group; others have a strong sense of separate social identity and resist acculturation in a variety of ways.

Work by social psychologists (notably, Tajfel, 1977, 1978, 1982; Tajfel & Turner, 1979) in the area of inter-group relations is clearly relevant for an understanding of this diversity of response. Tajfel (1974), for instance, describes a sequence of social categorization — social identity — social comparison — psychological distinctiveness which every individual undergoes. Our identity is determined by a knowledge of the different social categories to which we belong and the value which is attached to them. This identity is acquired through comparison with other groups. If we perceive our own group to be distinct from other groups and feel it compares favourably with them, we have an adequate social identity. If, however, our group compares unfavourably with others then we will be forced to seek a more positive identity in one of a number of quite distinct ways.

If, for instance, we accept our inferior status as fair and just and brought about by our own efforts and abilities, or the lack of them, the only way forward is by individualistic means. One solution is to compare oneself favourably with other members of the subordinate group; another possibility is to attempt to dissociate oneself from the subordinate group and gain acceptance as a member of the dominant group. If, however, we do not accept the justice of our low status, the response must necessarily be in the form of group rather than individual strategies. It is possible, for instance, to *redefine* group attributes which have previously been devalued as positive characteristics; or to seek direct competition with the outgroup; or to attempt complete assimilation.

Various writers (cf. Giles, 1977b; Taylor, 1980) have demonstrated the centrality of language in any discussion of inter-group relations. Ethnic markers in speech can be increased in order to maximize the social distance between speakers or reduced in order to minimize the distance (cf. Giles' theory of speech accommodation, discussed in Chapter 9) and thus play a critical role in the modelling of social identity. If, for instance, individuals accept their inferior status and attempt to pass to the superior group, this process will be marked linguistically by upward convergence in speech, as in the case of Mexican Americans who abandon the use of Spanish in favour of English (cf. Ryan & Carranza, 1977). If, however, they do not accept their low status position, and choose to redefine their group attributes in a more positive light, they are likely to accentuate these attributes through downward speech divergence. The Welsh language movement, Cymdaithas yr Iaith Cymraeg, is an example of one group which has taken this course. In the context of the present study, there is every reason to expect that the diversity of social identities which is to be found in young British Black people will be reflected in their linguistic behaviour.

Summary

The socio-economic situation of black people in Britain forms the focus for the present chapter which traces the recent history of black migration and the considerable body of evidence of racial discrimination. It also considers the statistics which point to the educational underperformance of black children and the various responses of the school in this area. Early formulations of the problem suggested that a poor self-concept played an important part in this process; more recently it has been suggested that a more satisfactory explanation lies in institutional racism and larger societal issues concerning the treatment of black people.

The varying responses of black people to the realities of racial inequality are considered. Attempts to describe these responses tend to fall into two main groups: those which treat black people as an undifferentiated, homogeneous whole, and those which attempt finer categorizations. Both approaches have been criticized for obscuring the nature and extent of diversity in the black community. It is argued that an appreciation of these different responses is likely to be extremely important for an understanding of any differences which may emerge in the language behaviour of black people.

3 Issues in the study of Black Language in Britain

Caribbean and British varieties of English differ systematically in phonology and grammar. The arrival of West Indians in Britain created a very interesting language contact situation which presented a wide range of challenges for descriptive linguists, sociolinguists and social psychologists. It is astonishing that so few researchers have been attracted by the study of this area. Very little systematic research has been undertaken, and much of our information comes from MA dissertations or theses which suffer from the inevitable shortcomings of small scale research. Work which has been done to date falls into six main categories: language attitudes; the sociology of language; educational policy; Patois interference; verbal skills; and description. In order to set the scene for the present study, each of these areas will be discussed in turn.

Attitudes towards West Indian speech

There is a long tradition of negative attitudes towards non-standard speech and only in recent times have attempts been made to explain different varieties in terms of social and historical development, rather than as a result of laziness or stupidity. West Indians in the Caribbean, educated on the British model, have been taught that they speak "bad talk" and that they will never amount to anything unless they learn to use standard English, though Patois remains the language of sincerity and is reserved for expressing strong emotion (cf. Reisman, 1970). Similarly, negative emotions have long existed in Britain towards non-standard speech and it is not surprising that attitudes towards Patois should have proved to be unfavourable when West Indians began settling in this country. Although there has been little empirical research in this area, negative attitudes towards Patois can frequently be detected in the education literature.

Reactions in the educational world to language need to be considered in the context of the debate which raged in many parts of the English speaking world in the 1960s on the subject of whether non-standard varieties were deficient or merely different. Many educationalists influenced by the work of Bernstein, or, in some cases, a misinterpretation of the work of Bernstein, felt that non-standard speakers were restricted by their language and linked alleged linguistic deficiencies with cognitive deficiencies (Hess & Shipman, 1965; Bereiter & Engelmann, 1966; Blank, 1970). This position has been strongly criticized by linguists (see J. Edwards, 1979; Gordon, 1981, for a review of this area) who have demonstrated that non-standard varieties are just as regular, flexible and logical as the standard.

However, misconceptions which were prevalent at this time no doubt explain comments made by some of the contributors to the report produced by the Birmingham branch of the Association of Teachers of English to Pupils from Overseas (ATEPO, 1970) on West Indian pupils. West Indian language is described as "babyish", "careless and slovenly", "lacking proper grammar" and even "very relaxed like the way they walk". There is a "glut of speech" but a "poverty of correct expression". Children are even reputed to communicate by sign language.

A report by the National Association of School Masters issued during this same period (NAS, 1969: 5) refers to West Indian language as a kind of "plantation English which is socially unacceptable and inadequate for communication".

The Concept 7–9 project and materials (Wight & Norris, 1970; Wight, 1969, 1970) can also be seen to some extent as a weak statement of the verbal deprivation hypothesis. Originally, the materials were envisaged as a language course for West Indian children. Later, however, it was decided that many of the language skills which they aimed to develop with West Indian children would also be useful for a good number of indigenous British children. Although they accepted that the language of non-standard English speaking children was perfectly adequate in its own right, and that no attempts should be made to change their speech, they considered that these children needed to develop a whole range of *verbal strategies* which would help them to compete on more equal terms in school.

Sutcliffe (1978) and V. Edwards (1979) point to the weakness in this position. They draw attention to the fact that no reference has been made to the children's language outside the classroom, and argue that the strategies which the materials were designed to promote may already be present in their speech. Certainly American research (see, for instance, Houston, 1973) has demonstrated that the deficiencies which intervention programmes were seeking to remedy did not exist when chldren's language was studied in a wide range of situations. It would seem highly probable that the most satisfactory explanation of why children do not use particular verbal strategies in the classroom — and this is far from certain — lies in terms of situational constraints rather than an inability to do so. Recent work by Tizard & Hughes (1984) on the language of young children at home and at school also supports this interpretation.

The danger of ignoring situational constraints is well illustrated by Pollack (1972) in her study *Today's Three Year Olds in London*. She remarks on the astonishingly small number of West Indian children who knew their own names and sex and, because of their lack of response to the first line of a children's rhyme, she concludes that West Indians have no tradition of nursery rhymes. The West Indian oral tradition does in fact include both English and more specifically West Indian nursery rhymes (cf. Elder, 1973; Conolly *et al.*, 1981). Since there is no evidence to support the notion that West Indian children are verbally deprived, we can only seek an explanation for their poor interview performance in terms of situational variables. (Might the children feel it was more polite to remain silent than to reply when faced with an unknown adult? Is the little girl wearing her best dress and with her hair plaited incredulous at being asked if she is a girl or a boy?)

V. Edwards (1978a) argues that negative attitudes to language rather than linguistic deprivation may be responsible in part for the underperformance of West Indian children in British schools, and suggests that there are strong links between attitudes towards language and attitudes towards speakers of that language. Student teachers, British middle and working class children and British Black children listened to taped extracts of a working class Reading boy, a middle class boy, a recently arrived Jamaican girl and a British born Barbadian girl who, unbeknown to the "judges", spoke twice, once in a Reading dialect and once in a Bajan dialect. A hierarchical situation emerged from the judges' evaluations in which the middle class boy was looked upon most favourably, followed by the working class speakers and then by the West Indian speakers. Significantly, the same child was evaluated more positively when she spoke with an English accent than when she used a West Indian one. Some of the student teacher judges also considered that the West Indian girls would do worse academically and be less interesting members of the class. Although it is impossible to predict how teachers will behave in the classroom towards West Indian or other minority group children, Edwards points to the danger that they will convey these negative feelings to the children.

Breinburg (in press) also supports the notion that teacher attitudes are more critical than children's language *per se*. She argues that it is the manner in which teachers perceive black children which is the main issue in their educational underperformance, and that the positions of both "deficit" and "difference" theorists have little relevance for this debate.

"Interference" or "Influence"?

Linguistic interference is another theme which appears in the literature. Like the discussions of language attitudes which we have just considered, studies of linguistic interference are set against an educational backcloth. Language was identified as one of the areas which was effectively holding children back and there was both concern and confusion about the ways in which teachers should respond (cf. ATEPO, 1970, Townsend, 1971). The first serious attempts to describe the language of West Indian children owed a great deal to contrastive analysis (cf. Lado, 1957) and were very much in the tradition of linguistic interference.

Interference was an important theme in linguistics during this period. Weinreich (1968) produced the first extensive discussion on this area, defining interference as "those instances of deviations from the norms of either language which occur in the speech of bilinguals as a result of their unfamiliarity with more than one language". In the early days of immigration educationalists assumed that West Indian children would rapidly assimilate the language of their British peers. As it became apparent that the language of many West Indian children remained quite distinct from local white usage, the theory of linguistic interference offered a useful mechanism for investigating the extent and degree of this difference.

It is possible to object to the notion of linguistic interference on the grounds that it attempts to define a person's language only with reference to another language, rather than describing it in its own terms. The theory of interlanguage (cf. Selinker, 1972), a later development, is more acceptable in this respect. The speaker's attempts to produce a target language are seen as complete languages, rather than as restricted versions of another language, inasmuch as they are rule governed, express meaning more or less adequately, and can be varied according to the situation. However, it is important to understand that those who used a linguistic interference approach always maintained that the speakers' original language or dialect was perfectly adequate in its own right and thus took issue with proponents of linguistic deprivation. The motivation for the interference studies in a British context was to show the ways in which Patois differed systematically from standard English, a very necessary step in the education of teachers who often dismissed non-standard varieties as "bad" or "sloppy".

Certain British educationalists (e.g. Wight, 1976; Goody, 1981) have found the notion of interference extremely disturbing. There seems to have been a widespread anxiety that it might be seized upon as a scapegoat in attempts to explain the educational underperformance of black children, enabling teachers to place the blame on the children themselves and thus divert attention from institutional factors which may be contributing to low achievement. While sympathizing with this position, it is important to remember that all the studies which identify linguistic interference stress that there is considerable variation from speaker to speaker, and that none suggests that Patois interference is the sole or even the main factor in the educational underperformance of West Indian children.

It is interesting to speculate to what extent the negative connotations attached to "interference" in common parlance may have influenced evaluations of the phenomenon. There are no reports of unfavourable reactions to dialect interference from educationalists in the Netherlands, for instance, where the technical term interference is translated as interferentie and the everyday expression as bemoeïen. Perhaps more considered responses would have been forthcoming if linguistic studies had consistently referred to Patois "influence" rather than "interference".

"Interference" studies

V. Edwards (1980) reviews a wide range of studies which discuss the issue of dialect interference. Earlier studies (e.g. Wight & Norris, 1970; Petrie, 1972; Baker, 1976; V. Edwards 1976, 1978b) consistently show the influence of Patois on children's speech, reading comprehension and writing. Later studies show conflicting trends, particularly in the area of reading. Anderson (1979) corroborates the earlier findings of V. Edwards (1975) that West Indian children's reading comprehension is affected by the extent to which they are influenced by Patois. Smolins (1974), Phillips (1978) and Pumfrey & Lee (1982), however, can find no evidence for any such effect. It is very difficult to make comparisons between the two groups of studies because of the very different conditions under which testing was carried out. Smolins and Phillips work with younger children who, for the greatest part, do not achieve the reading levels for which Edwards and Anderson predict difficulty. The Pumfrey & Lee study, on the other hand, deals with British born children, while both Anderson and Edwards consider a mixture of Caribbean and British born children.

One of the consequences of immigration legislation enacted in the 1960s is that, since 1970, almost all children of West Indian parents have been born in Britain. The linguistic consequences of the transition from

West Indian to British Black are reflected in the fact that the number of studies of Patois influence on the production and comprehension of English has dramatically reduced. The majority of these children would now appear to be able to speak a form of English largely indistinguishable from that of their white peers. Dialect interference is thus a theme which rarely appears in the literature any more. However, Lander (1979) confirms that the writing of 10–12 year old British Black children was further removed from standard English than that of other British children of comparable background, while Wright (1984), finds varying degrees of influence from Jamaican Patois in tests of the comprehension and production of standard English passives by British born male adolescents.

Studies in the sociology of language

Throughout the 1970s the number of black children who could speak a variety of English very close to or indistinguishable from the local white norm grew considerably. The presence of these children gave rise to a number of interesting questions about patterns of language use. Sutcliffe (1978; 1982a), for instance, administered a questionnaire in structured group interviews to 47 British and Caribbean born West Indians. Only 2% of the sample claimed that they used no Patois at all while 88% of the Caribbean born and 79% of the British born said that they used Patois of a broadness equivalent to: *mi aks di man fi put mi money eena im pockit.* Similar results were achieved by Hadi (1976) who used a modified form of the questionnaire in a project with first year children in a multiracial comprehensive school in the Midlands. Over 70% of the West Indians said that they sometimes used Patois of a broadness equivalent to "mi aks di man . . . .".

It is difficult to reconcile the findings of Sutcliffe and Hadi with those of Rosen & Burgess (1980) in an investigation of some 4,600 pupils between the ages of 11 and 12 in 28 London schools. Responses to questions completed by teachers on the language use of children of West Indian origin suggested that as few as 20% of children of Jamaican origin (and 10% of children whose parents come from Eastern Caribbean territories) have Jamaican (or other Caribbean creoles) as their dominant speech, or use it regularly in certain contexts, while 80% of Jamaican children (and 90% of children from other Caribbean territories) are basically London or standard speakers who occasionally "deepen" the dialect features.

All the studies drew on male and female speakers. Hadi's speakers were the same age as those in the Rosen & Burgess sample but behaved in the same way as the slightly older children in the Sutcliffe study. It is also doubtful whether location was responsible for the divergent findings, since all three studies took place in different parts of the country. The most likely explanations for the reported differences would thus seem to be in terms of methodology. Rosen & Burgess required teachers to select one of the following possibilities:

— The pupil is basically bidialectal and speaks the overseas dialect regularly in certain contexts.
— The overseas dialect is the pupil's dominant dialect.
— Basically a London (or standard) speaker, but occasionally deepens the overseas dialectal features in certain contexts or for certain effects.

Hadi and Sutcliffe, on the other hand, give children an actual example with which to compare their own language use. They also establish their own positive feelings about linguistic diversity by playing and discussing tapes of West Indian speech, and they thereby set up a context of assumed shared knowledge. Given the very low status of Patois and the ambivalence of West Indian speakers discussed above (see *Attitudes to West Indian Speech*), it seems highly probable that the discussions between teachers and pupils on which assessments were based would be more likely to produce under-reporting than a technique which offers children a more objective anchor point for assessing — and legitimizing — their own language use.

Palmer (1981) adds weight to this interpretation with an attempt to compare the methodologies used by both sets of researchers. First she replicated the Rosen & Burgess methodology by locating a well-motivated teacher of 10 to 11 year old children and discussing with him how their questionnaires should be completed. When this part of the exercise was over, she visited the class herself and, after playing and discussing tapes of various languages and dialects, she withdrew small groups of children and administered the Sutcliffe questionnaire. Children's self-estimates of Patois usage were consistently higher than those of the teacher, although he had consulted the children before completing the questionnaire.

The possibility of under-reporting is further supported by the findings of Tomlin's (1981) study of a random sample of West Indian speakers in Dudley. 100% of the young people under the age of 25 who took part in street interviews claimed that they regularly used Patois in some situations. Significantly, both the interviewers who took part in this study were black. In contrast, however, Breinburg (1983), a Surinamese writer, reporting the findings of a research project on young black people in a number of European cities, concludes that there is ample evidence that large numbers of youths speak neither the standard language nor a creole, but the local non-standard white dialect. She does, however, mention both "macaroni" (rapid switching between English and Patois) and domain-specific language variation. The picture concerning the extent of Patois usage thus remains extremely unclear.

Other studies in the sociology of language try to identify characteristics of the speaker which correlates with Patois usage. Crump (1979), for instance, attempts to relate the language varieties of black adolescents to their involvement in particular youth cultures. Children's comments, together with observations of the classroom and playground in the Haringey comprehensive school where she works, lead her to suggest that it is only when pupils develop an orientation to one or another of the major youth cultural groupings that differences in language use become apparent. In her experience, those pupils who by the third and fourth years use Patois and take pride in "talking black" are those who turn to the all black world of reggae and sound systems.

Leitch (1979a) a Guyanese writer, draws on her "inside" knowledge of the British Black community to present a profile of factors which she considers affect the language of British born children. These factors include where in the Caribbean their family comes from; the social background of the family; how long they or their family have lived in Britain; and, most important, the proportion of people with whom they associate who are of Caribbean origin and who speak a Patois, and the extent to which they identify with Caribbean or British culture. In her observation, the language of these children is also influenced by the Patois or other language of their parents; peer group language; language of the school and media; London Jamaican; and Rastafarian language.

The symbolic function of Patois is explored by Thomas (1979) in an ethnographic report based on participation-observation in a multi-ethnic primary school. She develops the metaphorical construct of "personal space" which she conceives in terms of "territory" that can be infringed or vindicated in the course of interaction. She suggests that it is possible to interpret the use of Patois in the classroom in a number of ways: it can act as a reinforcement of group communication; it can exclude an outsider who violates their personal space; or it can signify inclusion if they wish to include an outsider.

Sutcliffe (1978; 1982a) extends our understanding of Patois usage from the peer group to the family. It has often been assumed that Patois is reserved for interaction in the home and English for other settings, but this would appear to be a gross simplification of what actually takes place. Children questioned on their language behaviour reported a low use of

Patois to parents and siblings and a high use of Patois from parents to children and in the peer group. There would seem to be a widespread expectation that younger people should use "English" to their parents and even older brothers and sisters, but parents and older siblings are allowed to use "Patois" to their juniors. This practice would appear to be similar in many respects to the use of *tu* and *usted* in Spanish or, *tu* and *vous* in French a generation or so ago.

Educational policy

Suggestions regarding educational policy can be divided broadly into two: those concerning the acquisition of standard English by West Indian and other non-standard English speakers, and those concerning the use of Patois in a school setting. As regards the acquisition of standard English, there seems to be an increasingly strong climate of opinion that it is counter-productive to "correct" dialect features in speech, reading or writing. There is certainly consensus that no attempt should be made to change children's speech at any point in their school career (Wight, 1971; Leitch, 1979b). The links between language and identity are so strong that any attempts to impose standard English are likely to meet with strong resistance and will be interpreted as an act of rejection by the child.

The Dialect Kit of the Concept 7–9 materials is designed to teach West Indian children standard written English, but it is very doubtful if this can be achieved either by the means advocated in the Concept 7–9 materials or by the constant correction and criticism of non-standard features which is still, regrettably, a feature of many classrooms. It has been suggested, for instance, that "correction", because of its *ad hoc* nature, may very well lead to linguistic insecurity and hypercorrection (V. Edwards, 1979; Cheshire, 1982).

The whole question of Patois interference in writing is put into perspective by Richmond (1979) who offers a very interesting analysis of Pat, a second generation Jamaican girl in her third year of secondary school. Adopting the simple system of indicating errors, miscues and confusions (EMCs) in grammaticality, meaning, punctuation and spelling with numbers, and non-standard features with letters, he shows that EMCs occur four times as frequently as non-standard features in examples of Pat's work. Underlining the links between language and identity, he suggests that teachers should concentrate on ways of teaching writing which are unrelated to dialect. If dialect features are still to be found in the work of fourth year pupils it should be possible to point out those features and their standard English equivalents and to provide information about the existence of many dialects within a language if this has not already been done.

There are also strong arguments against "correcting" dialect features in children's oral reading. Reading researchers see the reading process as heavily dependent on the systems of various kinds which allow us to predict what lies ahead and to confirm or modify these predictions as we proceed (Gollasch, 1982; Smith, 1978). Dialect influenced children who read *He come home* for *He came home* are demonstrating very healthy reading strategies, since they are drawing on knowledge of their language to predict what comes next and have clearly understood what the writer intended to communicate. Following Goodman & Buck (1973), Wight (1976), V. Edwards (1979; 1983) and Leitch (1979b) suggest that the teacher who corrects dialect features is encouraging the child to read for accuracy and not for meaning. It may well be that the rejection of dialect by the school is an important factor in reading failure.

Until recently, most attention has been focussed on the route to the acquisition of standard English and little discussion has taken place on the ways in which Patois (and other non-standard speech) can be used to some considerable effect in the classroom. V. Edwards (1979) describes the very successful efforts of a number of teachers to use Patois, and argues that, paradoxically, children are more likely to be motivated to learn the standard when teachers use a bidialectal approach, in which both standard and non-standard English are given status in the classroom and the standard is presented as more appropriate in certain contexts. Further initiatives in this direction are described by the Talk Workshop Group (1982), and Open University (1985).

Changes in the attitude towards non-standard speech clearly have important implications for curriculum development. Rosen & Burgess (1980), for instance, argue that linguistic diversity of all kinds could be used as the core of language study. Language awareness programmes of this kind have also been proposed by Hawkins (1984) and Stubbs & Hillier (1983) and have particularly important implications for Patois speakers. Whereas Urdu, Polish and many other heritage languages have been introduced into the curriculum as examination subjects, this option has never been seriously available to Patois, partly because of problems of standardization and partly because of the lack of community demand. In the context of language awareness programmes, however, Patois can be presented as a valid linguistic system in its own right, thus dispelling myths of inferiority (cf. Sebba & White, forthcoming). Until recently teachers have tended to view the idea of introducing non-standard dialects into the classroom as incompatible with teaching children the standard which they believe gives access to educational success and social mobility. The work of Rosen & Burgess and others reviewed above thus represents a very important development. Non-standard speech is seen as a source of strength on which the teacher can build, not as something which is to be eliminated at all costs.

This suggestion has met a good deal of resistance in some quarters. V. Edwards (1979) reports the case of one headmaster who would "create a black curriculum" or "put Patois on the timetable" only over his dead body. It is certainly true that teachers tend to create an unnecessary polarization in terms of either the standard or the non-standard, and find it difficult to understand that the use of dialect in the classroom need in no way adversely affect the teaching of the standard. There are also objections from within the black community. Stone (1981), for instance, points to the symbolic role of Patois as a language of resistance and suggests that any attempts to introduce it into the curriculum are bound to fail. Carby (1980) objects on the ground that discussions of language divert attention from the racism present in school and society.

While attempts to introduce Patois as a school subject on the same level as French or German would understandably be doomed to failure, it is doubtful whether initiatives on the scale suggested by Rampton (1981) are likely to provoke unfavourable pupil reactions. Certainly those teachers currently involved in projects of this kind report enthusiastic rather than hostile responses (cf. V. Edwards, 1979; 1983). It is also possible to argue that, while language awareness programmes cannot change the society outside school, they can be a very useful instrument in anti-racist teaching, since they attack a number of myths and stereotypes about non-standard language.

Verbal skills

A great deal is said in the literature about what many children do not have (*viz* standard English) while very little attention is paid to what they do have (*viz* a lively oral tradition and wide range of verbal skills). An impressive catalogue of research has been compiled in the USA about the verbal skills of speakers of Black English Vernacular, a variety which has many points of similarity with West Indian Patois (see, for example, Whitten & Szwed, 1970; Kochman, 1972). There has also been some very interesting research on verbal skills in the West Indies (Reisman, 1970, 1974; Abrahams, 1972a,b).

Far less work has been undertaken in Britain, although there is a growing awareness of the importance of this area. Sutcliffe (1976), for instance, gives examples of folk tales and a heightened narrative style (known as rapping or styling by black Americans) from recordings of children in Bedfordshire. A far broader discussion of verbal skills is contained in Sutcliffe (1982a), while the specific question of black narrative style is considered in Sutcliffe (1982b). V. Edwards (1979) describes riddles and proverbs, taunting and teasing, story telling and reggae. Sutcliffe & Tomlin (in press) provide an analysis of black preaching style, testimony and prayer in church and their relation to the patterning of black communication styles in general.

Descriptive studies

Descriptive studies are also under-represented in the literature. The first serious description of the language of any group of West Indians in Britain was Wells' (1973) *Jamaican Pronunciation in London*, a study of adaptations to British norms made by some 36 respondents who had migrated as adolescents or adults. The next large scale research in this area dealt with both immigrant and British born children in Bedfordshire. Sutcliffe (1978) selected 32 extracts from a pool of recordings and ordered them on a continuum from Broad Patois to standard English according to certain phonological variables. It was possible in this way to illustrate the whole span of dialect encountered in the young black community. Although the dialect ranges along the continuum were wider than the literature suggests for Caribbean areas, there are strong indications that Patois remains an important force in the lives of many young British Blacks.

Sutcliffe (1982a) is the first to draw attention to the rapid switching from one part of the continuum to another which characterizes much British Black peer group speech. He argues that this switching is reminiscent of the in-group speech of bilinguals and confirms the autonomous status of Patois rather than in any way diminishing it. He supports this argument with comments from black speakers and an analysis of a short story written by Jennifer Johnson, a British born woman of Jamaican parents, all of which suggest that native speakers see a pattern beyond the variation and recognize the psychological reality of Patois. The autonomy of Patois is also underlined, along with the non-European input in its formation, in Carter (1982) and Sutcliffe (1982c). Jointly working on British-based data, they show Jamaican Patois to be a form of tonal language in which tonal patterns are associated with supra-segmental units, and may in fact signal grammatical distinctions.

Sutcliffe (forthcoming), drawing on the same data base used in the present study, addresses the problems posed for description by code-switching behaviour. He argues that, given a particular speaker and situations, where ethnicity and formality are controlled, language choice then depends on the roles that Patois and English play, concurrently, in at least three different spheres: discourse strategy; cultural symbolism (referencing black or white cultural worlds); and mood (ritual or non-ritual, dramatic or non-dramatic).

Sebba and associates (Sebba, 1984b, c, in press; Local, Wells, & Sebba, 1985; Sebba & Le Page, 1983; Sebba & Wootton, 1984), are also concerned with the question of code-switching. Two main language varieties — London Jamaican and Black London English — are distinguished. Both varieties differ in certain subtle respects from the varieties with which they are most closely associated. For instance, London Jamaican, unlike the Caribbean variety, would seem to retain certain characteristically English consonant clusters and to prefer *a* to *wan* as the singular indefinite article. Black London English restructures the complementizer system to include the use of *seh* after psychic state transitive verbs. Sebba & Wootton (1984) suggest that the most promising way to account for code-switching between these two varieties is on the basis of conversation-internal criteria. They show the ways in which switches from London Jamaican to Black London English often correspond to a change from the main theme in the conversation to some kind of sub-routine or secondary material; and how switches from Black London English to London Jamaican give added emphasis, particularly when ending an exchange.

The discussion up to this point, and indeed for the rest of the book, is restricted to English based Caribbean Creoles. It should be remembered, however, that French based Creoles are also to be found in the West Indies in Saint Lucia and Dominica and, to a much lesser extent, in Grenada and Trinidad. In the region of 17% of West Indian settlers came from these four islands in the first decade of migration (Peach, 1969), and probably less than half this proportion would have spoken a French based Creole. The research preoccupation with English based creoles in the British situation thus reflects the numerical preponderance of these groups rather than their intrinsic interest, and readers who wish to find out more about French based Caribbean creoles should consult Dalphines (1982; in press) and Kenrick (1982).

Where next?

A number of points emerge from this survey of the literature on black language in Britain. There is a good deal of confusion as to the proportion of British born black people who regularly use Patois and estimates vary from 10 (Rosen & Burgess, 1980) to 100% (Tomlin, 1981). Among those speakers who claim to use Patois there would seem to be a considerable variation in the degree of fluency achieved, but there is little documentation of the nature of this variation. It is now acknowledged that in-group speech is marked by frequent switches from "Patois" to "English" and a promising start has been made in the description of this code-switching behaviour.

Patois emerges as a low status variety which is heavily stigmatized in schools and in white society as a whole. It also clearly functions as a language of resistance for some sections of the black community. There is widespread recognition of the strong links between language and identity, and it is commonly assumed that only those young people who identify with black youth culture openly take pride in "talking black". There is a dearth of information, however, about other factors which may influence the use of Patois. Such information is critical for our understanding of the dynamics of language use in the black community and also has important implications for decisions about the use of Patois in school.

It is evident that a great deal more work needs to be done before we can claim to understand patterns of language use among British Black people. Many of the studies are speculative and are based on self-reports, or assertions about the nature of language use which have little or no empirical foundation. Sometimes observers have "insider" status within the British Black community; more frequently they do not and, all too often, they risk imposing an interpretation on events which diverges sharply from the community view of what is taking place. There are also important methodological weaknesses in many of the existing studies. Sample sizes are sometimes too small for the researcher to make interesting and valid generalizations; situational constraints are often overlooked; findings are sometimes confused by treating British and Caribbean born children as a homogeneous group.

If we are to arrive at a clearer picture of black language in Britain, the most obvious and pressing need is for a sociolinguistic study which describes patterns of language use and seeks to relate these patterns to the social processes which give rise to them. A prerequisite for such a study is a substantial corpus of data which draws on the speech of a wide range of British Black people in a wide range of situations. An important start in this direction has been made by Sutcliffe's description of the speech of young black people in Bedfordshire, but this study is more centrally linguistic than sociolinguistic and does not attempt an analysis in terms of origin (Caribbean or British), sex, education or any other background variable. Sebba's work on London Jamaican is also primarily in the descriptive linguistic mould and pays relatively little attention to the background of individual speakers. An adequate understanding of black language will need to draw on both descriptive and sociolinguistic studies.

Summary

Most discussion of black language in Britain has been set against an educational backcloth and a great deal of attention has been paid to the problems posed by language differences. Much of our present information in this area is based on self-reports of black children, and speculation. Most existing research is small scale and fragmented; there are many inconsistencies and contradictions. A great deal of the work which has been done is based on both immigrant and British born black children, and it is sometimes difficult to determine the extent to which findings apply to both groups. Very little work has centred firmly on the speech of British born black people, and no study to date has done more than speculate on the extent to which various social factors influence the production of language.

In order to overcome the weaknesses of previous attempts to describe this area, it was decided to base the present study on a substantial corpus of speech which reflects the whole range of stylistic and individual variation in the Black community, and which draws on information about their social characteristics. It is only in this way that we can hope to explain any patterns which may emerge.

4 A sociolinguistic framework for analysis

We have considered in previous chapters the social and political position of black people in Britain and the nature and extent of diversity in this community. We have also looked at the work which has been undertaken in the area of black language in Britain, its limitations, and promising directions in which we may now proceed. However, descriptions of language in the West Indies are also pertinent to the present discussion. A central concern of Caribbean linguistics has been the formation of a theoretical framework which adequately accounts for the highly variable nature of West Indian speech. Various approaches to this issue will be considered, in order to justify the sociolinguistic model of description adopted for the present study. Finally, the relevance of two questions of theoretical importance to British Black speech data will be discussed. The first relates to the extent of syntactic variation in British Black speech; the second concerns the qualitative differences between variation in Caribbean and British settings.

Issues in Caribbean linguistics

The language spoken by West Indian immigrants to Britain in the 1950s and 1960s differed in many important ways from that of the host society. One of its most salient characteristics was the degree and kind of variation which was to be found. Most people spoke what they considered to be "English", though this differed in important respects from British English. However, they also had access to other varieties which were incomprehensible to British listeners. A central issue in Caribbean linguistics has been the description of the variation which characterizes West Indian speech. Over the years, progress in this area has made important contributions to our understanding of linguistic variation in other settings and has, in its turn, been informed by developments outside the Caribbean. An appreciation of issues in Caribbean linguistics in particular, and the description of variation in general, is clearly of considerable importance for the description of the patterns of language use in a British Black context.

Slaves were transported to the Caribbean from all over West Africa and they spoke a wide range of languages. Very few slaves had much contact with Europeans (cf. Alleyne, 1971), and the most immediate problem was to communicate with each other rather than with the planters and their families. Documentation for this period is sparse, but we can be confident that the linguistic development which took place in the Caribbean would have followed the same pattern which has been observed in many other situations of multilingual contact (cf. Todd, 1974). In the first generation, a pidgin would have evolved. Pidgins are very simplified forms of communication: vocabularies are small, there are very few grammatical rules, inflectional endings are lost and speakers rely heavily on gesture. If the situation which gave rise to the pidgin remains unchanged, important developments take place in subsequent generations as the pidgin is developed into a creole, a language in its own right. Whereas pidginization is marked by simplification, the hallmark of creolization is elaboration. A pidgin allows only limited communication but a creole, with its greatly expanded vocabulary and grammar, is capable of fulfilling all the speakers' needs.

In territories like Surinam where English colonists were replaced by the Dutch, a stable and autonomous variety known as Sranan emerged. Islands like Jamaica and Barbados, however, remained under British control and the linguistic consequences were quite different. Because of the continuing contact between English and the creole, a process of decreolization is taking place, resulting in what some writers (e.g. De Camp, 1971) have called a post-creole continuum linking the broadest variety of the creole with the local standard language. One of the peculiarities of this continuum is a far greater degree of variation than would normally be found in communities which have been subject to the usual processes of dialect formation, in which differences gradually diffuse through a population of speakers.

Linguistic models

One of the recurring themes in Caribbean linguistics is the formulation of the most appropriate theoretical framework for describing this variation. Early attempts to grapple with the question led to the assumption that it was possible to disentangle two distinct varieties, a standard or acrolectal variety which differs systematically, but in only a small number of areas, from standard British English; and a broad or basilectal variety which differs maximally from this standard. Bailey (1966, 1971), for example, considers

Jamaican Creole and standard Jamaican English to be the two systems which lie at the core of a co-structure. In this way she explains actual variation in terms of incursions either from the standard or from the creole.

The main difficulty with this formulation is that there are many forms and structures which can quite reasonably be assigned to both systems. There are also intermediate forms which fit neatly into neither system. Attention thus began to be focussed on more satisfactory ways of describing the variation which characterizes actual speech data. De Camp (1971), for instance, links the Creole and the standard in a linear continuum, using implicational scales in which the possession of one feature entails the possession of all other features below it in the hierarchy.

Bickerton (1973, 1975) uses the De Camp model as the basis of his "polylectal" grammar of language in Guyana. Implicational scales are used essentially as discovery tools which allow the linguist to produce a continuum of isolects, or self-contained grammars, which differ from each other in just one feature. Bickerton proposes that the current state of the Guyanese language represents a slice of an historical process in which the past is represented by the basilect and the future by the acrolect. He thus claims to break down the Saussurian dichotomy between synchronic and diachronic studies. There are various objections to implicational scaling (see, for instance, Hudson, 1980; Romaine, 1982b; Gibson, 1982; Le Page & Tabouret Keller, in press). The scaleability of variables which is central to this approach has been seriously questioned and doubts have also been expressed about the adequacy of a description which draws on linguistic — but not sociolinguistic — information.

Sociolinguistic models

Various alternatives have been proposed which aim to incorporate another dimension of description by taking into account social character-istics of the speaker. The pioneer of this approach to language was William Labov, and although speakers of American rather than Caribbean varieties have formed the focus of his studies, his work has important implications for Caribbean linguistics.

Central to the analysis which Labov developed is the notion of the linguistic variable. The variation in the pronunciation of phones in some words had previously received a great deal of attention in the literature. Some writers chose to describe this variation in terms of two alternating phonemic systems; others preferred to explain the alternation as shifts between allophones in the same system (see Joos, 1966). Labov preferred to treat such variation within a single system, and claimed that careful analysis of the speech behaviour of a community will reveal both phonemes and linguistic variables. Thus, in New York City, for instance, the pronunciations of dental fricatives and bilabial stops will all cluster around definable articulation peaks; the pronunciation of the vowel found in words like *bad*, however, can vary along a four point scale from most standard to least standard.

The usefulness of the linguistic variable lies in the possibilities which it offers for quantification of speech data and correlation with background variables such as sex, education and social class. Although various difficulties have been noted by other researchers attempting to apply this methodology (see, for instance, Romaine, 1982a), it allowed Labov to make extremely useful generalizations about the effects of age, sex, social class and style on language use. His findings have subsequently been confirmed in a number of studies in the same tradition, most notably Shuy, Wolfram & Riley (1968) in Detroit and Trudgill (1974) in Norwich.

The Labovian model represented a quantum leap in linguistic theory. However, it raises a wide range of problems when applied to Caribbean data. It assumes, for instance, that all members of a given speech community share a grammar in such a way that divergent dialects are derived from a common underlying grammar. Le Page (1975) points out that such a position is untenable for creole communities where, as the result of exposure to education, speakers *add* rather than delete rules, as Labov suggests. Certain of the social assumptions which Labov makes are also problematic. His concept of social class may be both relevant and meaningful in the context of American societies, but is unhelpful when applied to a whole range of other settings, including the Caribbean.

It is true that social class assumes a central importance in Labov's work. He argues, for instance, that we all follow the overt norms of the speech community in formal situations, and that these norms usually coincide with the speech of the highest socio-economic class, because of their social prestige. He also proposes that individuals emulate the speech of those in the socio-economic classes above them, and this formulation has important implications for his explanations of language change. It is possible, however, to use Labovian methodology without necessarily accepting every aspect of his theoretical stance. In its most basic form it simply entails the correlations of certain selected linguistic variables with social characteristics of the speaker. For instance, writers like Escure (1979, 1981, 1982, 1983a, b, 1984, in press) have used social categories such as ethnicity to provide extremely illuminating insights on the question of language variation in Belize.

Le Page suggests an alternative to Labovian theory in the form of a multi-dimensional model of language which gives priority to the socio-linguistic motivation of a speaker in language choice. Central to this view of language behaviour are the processes of "projection" and "focussing" in which all speakers engage:

> "We engage in activities I call projection and focussing: we project on to the social screen the concepts we have formed, by talking about them, so as to furnish our universe and try to get others to acknowledge the shape of the furniture; we in turn try to bring our concepts into focus with those of others, so that there is a feedback from the screen through language. A child who identifies easily with the stereotypes or concepts of a monolingual society will have a highly focussed language system; the children I have been con-cerned with, in Belize or St. Lucia or the immigrant Sikh children in Leeds, have much more diffuse systems" (1975: 12)

He proposes that linguistic behaviour is conditioned by the desire to identify with different groups. The success of our efforts is determined by the extent to which we are able to identify our model groups; the opportunity and ability to observe and analyse their behavioural systems; and the motivation and ability to adapt our behaviour in the direction of the model group. Like Labov, he isolates socially significant linguistic variables, but tries to avoid working with pre-determined social categories. Le Page's chosen analytical tool was cluster analysis. He attempted to determine which children are most alike behaviourally and which clusters they fall into on the basis of some 25 linguistic "quantities". Problems arose in the course of this analysis (McEntegart & Le Page, 1982; Le Page & Tabouret Keller, in press) which raised serious questions about the suitability of cluster analysis for socio-linguistic data. However, this in no way detracts from the value of his basic formulation of the nature of language behaviour.

Although the terminology is different, there are in fact many similari-ties between Le Page's model and that proposed by Milroy (1980). The central tenet of Milroy's approach is that the social networks, or informal and formal relationships which make up all human societies, are distin-guished by their own patterns of language use. Such an approach stresses social solidarity and the normative influence of the group on the language of its members. By identifying those relations which are important for the community she is describing, she is able to develop a network strength scale, and to demonstrate the ways in which network correlates with language use. Thus Milroy's view of the ways in which social relations affect language behaviour corresponds quite closely to the Le Page formulation. Both approaches concentrate on the individual rather than the group, and the importance of the individual's relationship with their own and other groups.

However, Milroy's network strength scale proves to be a far stronger analytical tool than Le Page's attempt at cluster analysis.

Milroy's work is based on the more "focussed" speech of working class communities in Belfast, but there is every reason to suppose that it will be equally successful in the analysis of more "diffuse" communities. One preliminary attempt has been made by W. Edwards (1984) who re-analyses part of the data collected in a sociolinguistic survey of urban and rural communities in Guyana (W. Edwards, 1975) in terms of the social networks of the participants. Network analysis has also been used with very interesting results in studies of a bilingual community in Austria (Gal, 1979) and the urbanization of rural dialects in Brazil (Bortoni de Figueiredo Ricardo, 1983).

The present framework for analysis

The present study necessarily builds on the insights of the writers whose work is reviewed above. It starts from the premises that language cannot be studied in a social vacuum and that the individual speakers rather than the pre-defined group must be the focus for investigation. Its aim is to detect regularities in the data and to determine whether and how these regularities are socially motivated. In this way it should be possible to arrive at an understanding of the language behaviour of black people in British society.

In order to describe the patterns of language use which emerged from the data, it was clear that a variety of measures would be required. A simple correlational study which attempts to establish any relationships between social and linguistic variables is an obvious starting point. Chapter 7 describes one such attempt. A number of frequently occurring features which vary along the same dimension in response to the same social constraints are isolated for analysis. A Patois index based on these variables is constructed and index scores are calculated for each speaker in each of the five situations recorded. In this way it is possible to examine the effects of formality and ethnicity on the frequency of Patois usage. A Patois frequency score, based on the mean index scores across the different situations, is used for more precise correlations with a wide range of background variables, including sex, education, attitudes towards mainstream white society and degree of integration into the British Black community. It is possible on the basis of this analysis to make a variety of statements about the relationship between the social characteristics and the language behaviour of the young black people in the sample.

However, an approach which concerned itself only with measures of frequency of Patois usage would have left unanswered several very important questions about British Black language. The data we collected suggested, for instance, that some of the participants who used Patois features relatively infrequently were nonetheless perfectly competent Patois speakers. This raised a number of issues. Is there evidence that some young people are more proficient Patois speakers than others? If so, are different patterns of features associated with different levels of proficiency, or are Patois features distributed at random across the speakers? Are different levels of competence related to the social characteristics of the speaker? The Patois competence scale, discussed in Chapter 8, extends the list of variables included in the Patois index from 11 to 20, and attempts to answer questions such as these.

One more important trend in the data deserves discussion. The Patois index scores show that some situations emerge as more "English" and others as more "Patois". This raises an extremely important question: what constitutes Patois usage? If it is possible to define a situation as either Patois or English on the basis of independent linguistic criteria, then it will be possible to look at patterns of language use across speakers. This course opens up a whole range of exciting possibilities. Are different patterns of language use associated with different social characteristics of the speakers? What is the symbolic function of Patois usage? Can the same conversational intent be signalled with different levels of competence in Patois?

The subject of language in a British Black community will thus be pursued on three quite separate but complementary fronts: frequency of Patois usage, competence in Patois and patterns of language choice. This course of action by no means exhausts the possibilities for either linguistic or sociolinguistic analysis. It neglects, for instance, the question of code-switching, and makes no attempt to consider the linguistic constraints or the sociological and psychological determinants of this behaviour. There are various reasons for this omission. It is quite feasible, for instance, to present a macro-linguistic picture of language use, independent of micro-linguistic considerations. Thus, the relationship between social and linguistic variation does not rely on an understanding of the internal constraints on variation. It should also be remembered that the approach used in the present study is largely quantitative and attaches considerable importance to the social orientation of the speaker. Such an approach does not transfer easily to an analysis of code-switching which is always dependent on the immediate context for its interpretation. The data collected for the present study will, in fact, form the focus for a forthcoming study of code-switching by David Sutcliffe which draws on a very different methodology.

Some peculiarities of British Black speech data

Two main issues arose in the analysis of Black British speech data which require special comment. The first concerns the kind of linguistic variables which were used; the second the qualitative differences between the kind of variation which takes place in British and Caribbean settings.

The linguistic variable

The early quantitative sociolinguistic studies (cf. Labov, 1966; Trudgill, 1974) were based entirely, or almost entirely, on the analysis of phonological variables. Gradually, however, the notion of the linguistic variable extended to morpho-phonemic (e.g. -ED deletion, Labov, 1972, Chapter Eight), morpho-syntactic (e.g. third person singular present tense -s, Cheshire, 1982) and syntactic variables (e.g. *ne* deletion in Montreal French, Sankoff & Vincent, 1977; *that* deletion in American English, Kroch & Small, 1978). Interest in syntactic variation has grown considerably in recent years (cf. Trudgill, 1978, Chapter One; Edwards, Trudgill & Weltens, 1984), but it must be conceded that the quantitative study of syntax is potentially more problematic than the study of phonology.

The most obvious disadvantage in using syntactic variables is the relative infrequency of their occurrence. Whereas tokens of a phonological variable are likely to be fairly numerous in even a relatively short stretch of speech, tokens of a syntactic variable will almost certainly be far fewer. It is even possible that there will be no occurrences at all. The difficulty of eliciting syntactic variables has also been discussed in the literature (cf. Rickford, 1975; Hudson, 1980: 46). This problem is particularly acute in monolingual communities where syntactic variation is usually restricted to a very small number of constructions. In multilingual communities, however, where we are dealing with two or more quite distinct varieties, or in communities in which we find a post-creole continuum, examples of syntactic variation are far more common.

The second area of difficulty which has been discussed in relation to syntactic variables is the requirement first proposed by Labov (1972: 271) that variants should be "identical in reference or truth value, but opposed in their social and/or stylistic significance". Given this condition, phonological variables which do not have referential meaning are clearly preferable to non-phonological variables which do, because of the attendant problems of demonstrating that these non-phonological variables "mean the same" if they are to be treated as evidence of variability.

This position has given rise to considerable controversy (e.g. Lavandera, 1978; Romaine, 1981). It is firmly based on the assumption of classic generative grammar that dialects of the same language are distinct surface realizations of the same underlying grammar (cf. Chomsky & Halle, 1968; King, 1969). It has been understood for some time now that it is possible to demonstrate that the grammars of the creoles in Caribbean communities are in many ways distinct from those of the related superstrate languages (Le Page, 1975; Bickerton, 1975). A good example of this phenomenon is offered by the different treatments of uninflected simple past tense forms offered by Labov (1972) and Le Page (1975). For Labov forms such as *He start the engine* or *Mary walk home* in the speech of Black American speakers can be explained in terms of a rule which deletes the (ED) past tense inflection. Le Page, in contrast, maintains that Caribbean speakers *add* rather than *delete* this ending as they come increasingly into contact with the standard language. Morpho-syntactic and syntactic variants for Caribbean speakers thus cannot be held to be options within the same system as, for instance, the choice of active or passive verb forms would be for standard English speakers.

Most of the discussions of linguistic variation involve the presence or absence of a single linguistic item. In discussions of West Indian speech data, however, we are also dealing with alternation between quite different linguistic items. This situation is by no means unique to the Caribbean. Coveney (1985), for instance, discusses the social and stylistic significance of various interrogative structures in French, while Harris (1984) considers the different aspect systems of Hiberno-English and standard English.

The extension of the sociolinguistic variable from phonological to morpho-syntactic and syntactic features is problematic only if one adheres to the principle that there should be semantic ties between variants. Various writers (e.g. Lavandera, 1978; Sankoff & Thibault, 1977; Dines, 1980) argue that the notion of semantic equivalence should be replaced with one of functional similarity. While it is essential that variants must in some way be the same, the notion of semantic equivalence should not be considered a necessary condition for the definition of the sociolinguistic variable. Coveney (1985) sums up the situation thus —

> "I think the crucial question is whether individuals (or groups, or communities) *use* two or more forms to express the same thing. If they do, then the forms may be considered variants of variables (for the individual, or group, or community) provided that they satisfy a number of other criteria. The fact that two variants can be analyzed as being parts of two different systems does not, in itself, mean that they cannot be *used equivalently* to express the same meaning."

This is the position which is adopted in relation to the isolation of linguistic variables for various studies of Caribbean speech data (see Winford, 1984, for an overview of this area) and also for the present study. Variants are differentially distributed across speakers and situations. Sometimes it is possible to demonstrate semantic ties between variants; on other occasions this is not possible. But on all occasions variants share a common function and are recognized by speakers as being socially significant.

Variation in British and Caribbean settings

The most usual characterization of variation in a Caribbean setting is in terms of a continuum ranging from broad Patois to the local standard. West Indian speech data make it clear that the cline between the two ends of the continuum cannot be accounted for simply in terms of the relative proportions of standard (or acrolectal) and broad Patois (or basilectal) forms (cf. Bickerton, 1975; Le Page, 1975). There are also intermediate forms which cannot reasonably be assigned to either pole. As we have seen, the presence of these mesolectal features makes it necessary to reject the two system analysis originally proposed by Bailey (1966) in favour of alternative approaches.

Although the notion of a continuum analysis is not without its critics (cf. Lawton, 1980; Le Page & Tabouret Keller, in press), it is at least possible to make a *prima facie* case for this approach when dealing with Caribbean data. In contrast, recent descriptions of variation in British Black speech have strongly favoured an analysis in terms of two separate systems rather than a continuum analysis. Sutcliffe (1982a), for instance, argues that, despite the existence of a phonological continuum, the language complex in the British Black community is best described as two systems on the morpho-syntactic level. Sebba (1984a, b, c, in press) also supports this position, and chooses to talk in terms of two separate varieties, London Jamaican and London English, rather than a continuum. This would therefore appear to be an important area of difference between Caribbean and British speech data.

The present study found compelling reasons for supporting this position. The differing socio-political conditions in Britain and the West Indies, for instance, suggest quite different linguistic outcomes. In the Caribbean, black people form the majority and, despite a strong correlation between skin colour and social status (cf. Lowenthal, 1972), they are nonetheless represented at all levels of the social hierarchy. With greater possibilities of social mobility, larger numbers of speakers have gained access to more standard speech, thus creating the necessary conditions for a linguistic continuum situation (cf. Alleyne, 1980).

In Britain, in contrast, black people for the most part belong to the working class. This is not to suggest that they form a homogeneous group and there is undoubtedly enormous variation between black people in education, aspirations, material wealth and other features which are often associated with social class. It is indisputable, however, that black immigrants to Britain were expected to occupy low status jobs (Peach, 1969), and that they have systematically been denied access to positions for which they are adequately qualified (Brown, 1984). British Blacks are a visible minority in a society where blackness is not generally perceived as an asset, and where language choice is far more likely to relate to ethnicity than to social class. The conditions which would seem to be necessary for the creation of a continuum situation are simply absent in the British setting.

The linguistic evidence supports this position. Close examination of British Black speech suggests that the situation is closer to that of a bilingual community than to the post-creole continuum which operates in the Caribbean. Code-switching behaviour, which has been reported as a regular feature of stable bilingual communities (Ure, 1974; Hernandez-Chavez et al., 1975; Kachru, 1978, Poplack, 1980) is certainly a common feature of much in-group speech (cf. Sutcliffe, 1982a, forthcoming; Sebba, 1984a, b, c, in press). Claims have also been made for discrete varieties and code-shifting behaviour in a Jamaican context (Lawton, 1980), but it is much easier to make this case in a British context, where the varieties are a good deal further removed.

In Jamaica, basilectal and acrolectal phonology differ in only a small number of areas (see Wells, 1982). In Britain, not only are we dealing with two phonological systems which differ in important respects, but distinct voice sets for the different varieties. The background features of speech, including pitch, tempo, loudness and timbre are quite different for British English and West Indian varieties, so that there can seldom be any doubt as to whether a speaker is using "English" or "Patois" on phonetic criteria alone.

Equally important, it is easier to separate the grammars of the different varieties in a British setting. Although it is possible to argue for a code-switching analysis of some Caribbean data, it is difficult to see how meso-lectal varieties can be handled in such a framework. In British Black data, however, it would appear that mesolectal forms are less problematic. There is a strong polarization between "English" and "Patois" in which the preferred Patois variants are most often basilectal features. In a Caribbean context, we would expect to find a whole range of alternative forms: in addition to *im a guo* and *he's going*, we would have to account for forms like *im going* and *he going*. It would be misleading to suggest that intermediate forms do not occur in our data. Nor is it the case that, when they do occur, they are any easier to analyse than comparable Caribbean data (cf. Sutcliffe, forthcoming). It is nonetheless true that young British Black people prefer in the main basilectal Patois variants.

Wright (1984) also draws attention to this pattern. She compares the story telling of Malcolm, a British born boy reported in Sutcliffe (1982a) with a traditional Anansi story recounted by Tania, a Jamaican girl whom she recorded in Kingston. Malcolm offers to retell a story making it "more Jamaican", and produces a highly focussed basilectal performance. Tania's story, in contrast, is linguistically much more diffuse: she uses basilect for Anansi, acrolect for Snake and predominantly mesolectal forms for the narrator. Jamaicans consulted by Wright consider this variation to be normal rather than idiosyncratic. However, Malcolm's passage was judged as unusual. Opinions were also expressed as to the stereotypical nature of British Black speech which was not felt to be "real Jamaican".

The task of analysis was therefore a good deal simpler than it might have been if we were dealing with Caribbean data. Comparisons were made between "Patois" and "English" forms. Intermediate forms which would have required sometimes arbitrary decisions as to whether they should be assigned to "English" or "Patois" were sufficiently few in number to be excluded from this analysis.

Summary

Issues which have emerged as important in the description of linguistic variation in general and Caribbean language varieties in particular have been discussed in order to explain the sociolinguistic framework for analysis which has been adopted for the present study. The assumption has been made that language cannot be studied in a social vacuum and that individual speakers rather than pre-determined groups should form the focus for study. Our approach to the study of British Black speakers thus builds on the insights of many prominent linguists, but owes a particular debt to network analysis and the work of Milroy (1980) and Gal (1979).

The different approaches to the analysis of British Black speech data in Chapters 7, 8 and 9 are outlined, and attention is drawn to some peculiarities in the data. One issue of interest is the nature of the linguistic variable. Most sociolinguistic analyses are based on phonological variation and some controversy exists as to the feasibility of an analysis of syntactic variants. It is argued that the theoretical basis for this position is unsound and that, in view of the considerable variation which exists in British Black speech, it is quite reasonable to consider a wide range of syntactic as well as morpho-syntactic and phonological variables.

A second issue relates to the nature of variation. It is suggested that variation in a British setting is qualitatively different from that found in the

Caribbean. West Indian speech is usually characterized as a continuum from broad Patois to the standard. Whereas the two poles of the continuum are fairly well defined, the intermediate stages are highly variable and very difficult to describe. British Black speakers, in contrast, tend to prefer polar variants and to avoid the intermediate forms. Their behaviour is thus far more reminiscent of that normally associated with a bilingual community than that of a post-creole continuum.

5 Composition of the sample

The British Black community encompasses a wide range of groups. In its broadest sense it includes West Indians, Africans, South Asians and other non-white ethnic minorities. However, the term "British Black" is most often restricted to people with direct or indirect links with the former British West Indies and this is the sense in which it is used in the present study. Those born in the Caribbean come from many different islands and on arrival in Britain were more likely to think of themselves as Jamaican, Trinidadian or Vincentian than West Indian. As the novelist Salkey (1969) explains, "The blanket term West Indian doesn't exist in the West Indies; it does in London, has to for protection's sake."

Those born in Britain are obviously cognizant of the values and expectations of their parents, but have also experienced life and school in Britain. In restricting the present study to this latter British born group we realize that we are describing *a* and not *the* British Black community. We also acknowledge the inevitable diversity which characterizes this particular community. Indeed this diversity and its possible effects on linguistic behaviour represent the starting point for study.

There are two prerequisites for a socially sensitive description of British Black language: first, we need to identify a sample of speakers who represent the groups and norms observed to be important within the community which is being studied; second, we need to record as wide a range as possible of these speakers' linguistic repertoires. The present chapter considers the problems associated with selecting a sample of speakers and describes the composition of the group of young people who took part in the study. Chapter 6 examines issues pertaining to the actual data collection.

Sampling methodology

One of the most important issues in discussions of research design is sampling methodology. There are two main alternatives. On the one hand, the researcher can work with a random sample. This has the advantage of ensuring that the speakers chosen are representative of the community as a whole, and the disadvantage of requiring large numbers of participants. On the other hand, the researcher can decide in advance, on the basis of careful observation, about the meaningful divisions in society, and draw on a smaller "judgement" or "quota" sample which reflects these divisions.

In studies of language, there is a strong preference for judgement samples, partly because linguistic behaviour seems to be more homogeneous than other kinds of social behaviour, so that increased data handling brings diminishing analytical returns; and partly because of the immense practical difficulties in working with large samples. Such samples can only be representative in a weak and non-technical sense. However, the very regularity and consistency of the relationships between language and social factors which they can detect, leave little doubt as to their validity (see Sankoff, 1980, and Milroy, forthcoming, for a fuller discussion of this area).

In a British Black context the only available option is to work with a judgement sample, because of the absence of ready-made sampling frames which enumerate the relevant population. The census, for instance, contains questions on country of birth, but not on language or ethnicity. This information is potentially useful in the case of first generation immigrants, but cannot help us to identify their British born children. Various alternative approaches have been devised. De Lange & Kosmin (1979), for instance, used name analysis methods in a study of the Jewish community; Leeuwenberg (1979), Singh (1979) and Chin & Simsova (1981) applied this same technique to Greek Cypriot, Sikh and Chinese communities respectively. The Linguistic Minorities Project (see, for example, G. Smith, 1984) used a variety of techniques, including name analysis and compilations of various community lists. The British Black population, however, cannot be identified by their names and are too large and heterogeneous a group to be reliably identified from community lists.

Even if sampling frames were readily available, it would be difficult to overcome the problems created by the non-random distribution of the black population. For historical reasons, black people tend to be found in a relatively small number of British cities, and to be further concentrated into a small number of locations within these cities. Equally important, the notion of social class is highly problematic in any discussion of the British Black community. Social class divisions are based on occupation, and their usefulness lies in the fact that occupation tends to be highly correlated with a wide range of structural factors, such as level of education and child rearing practices. However, for a variety of reasons, social class does not accurately indicate the same range of values and attitudes in black people as it does in whites.

When West Indians first settled in Britain they tended to accept jobs of a lower status than those which they held in the Caribbean (cf. Peach, 1969). D. Smith (1976) documents the continuing inequalities of black people in British society and the most recently available evidence (Brown, 1984) points to still further deterioration. Recruiting practices and employers' expectations tend to discriminate both directly and indirectly against black workers, and there is a considerable body of evidence which suggests that formal educational qualifications do not necessarily lead to the same level of work for black youth that they do for white youth (cf. Fuller, 1983; Jenkins & Troyna, 1983). Black people are thus artificially concentrated in the lower socio-economic groups and, not surprisingly, occupation is a poor index of values and attitudes for the British Black community.

The skewed distribution of British Black people, together with the absence of sampling frames, thus make it impossible to achieve a random, representative sample. Instead we have chosen to undertake a study of the linguistic repertoires of a particular group within the black community — young British born people — whose selection has been based on careful ethnographic observation of both the structural norms and values, and of the areas which unite and divide individuals within that community (cf. Blom & Gumperz, 1972). The description which follows is based on both the shared characteristics of the speakers in the sample (place of birth, residence, parents' island of origin and age) and those characteristics which differentiate speakers (sex, education, social network and attitudes towards mainstream white society).

Location

Participants in the study were British born black people living in Dudley, West Midlands. Dudley was chosen as the location for fieldwork, partly because two of the fieldworkers for the project live in this area and could take advantage of their social networks in making contact with speakers, and partly because this location allowed us to control the island of origin of the participants' parents, a potentially important variable in discussions of the British Black community. Although there are many common links in both language and patterns of language use between the various Caribbean territories, there are also important differences (see, for example, Le Page, 1957, 1958). The overwhelming majority of the black population of Dudley is of Jamaican origin, thus making the tasks of selecting participants and analysing their speech a good deal simpler. The choice of Dudley also has the useful effect of extending our knowledge of British Black language use from London (Rosen & Burgess, 1980; Sebba, 1984a, b, c, in press), Bedford (Sutcliffe, 1978) and Reading (V. Edwards, 1976) to a previously undocumented setting. The precaution was also taken to ensure that all speakers were British born, since we were not at all sure what effect, if any, varying degrees of residence would have on young people's speech.

Age

The speakers' age has been shown to be extremely important in explanations of language variation (cf. Labov, 1966; Milroy, 1980). In the context of a project on British Black English, however, patterns of migration have been such that the upper limit of the age range will be formed by subjects in their early twenties. It was decided to narrow this age range even further by including only subjects of 16 and over. There are a number of reasons for this decision. Various writers (e.g. Crump, 1979) refer to teacher reports that the speech of young black children closely resembles that of their white peers until about the ages of 14 or 15. At this point those who identify with the various black youth sub-cultures are reported to take pride in "talking black". It is probably not insignificant that the low rate of Patois usage reported in Rosen & Burgess (1980) relates to 12-year-old secondary school children who fall below this critical age.

This older group was also preferred for purely practical reasons. Any recording of younger children requires the permission and co-operation of parents or teachers, whereas older subjects are able to decide for themselves whether or not they wish to participate. Further, the formal distance between adult fieldworker and young children is such that speech can be easily inhibited (cf. Labov, 1969). Although this can be overcome by using radio microphones in play and family settings, it is considerably easier to enlist the services of young fieldworkers who can operate as participant-observers in peer group conversation.

Social distance attributable to age difference is not, of course, restricted to interaction between young children and adults. It would have been inappropriate to use older fieldworkers — white or black — with subjects in our selected age range in any attempt to elicit informal conversation. For this reason, a decision was made to work with fieldworkers of approximately the same age as the subjects themselves, except in the case of the formal white interview where the age difference between the participants was used to maximize the formality of the situation.

The young people who took part thus ranged in age from 16 to 23; were British born of Jamaican parents; and had lived in Dudley all or most of their lives. They differed in a number of important respects, however, which were to form the main focus for the present study. The sources of information on these differences were the growing sociological literature on the Black British community (e.g. Centre for Contemporary Cultural Studies, 1982; Cashmore & Troyna, 1982; Figueroa, 1982; Troyna & Smith, 1983), our own experience of ten years' work on black language in Britain; and the insights of the many young black people associated with the project. The various cultural variables which were selected for investigation are described below.

Sex of speaker

The variation of language with sex has been well documented (Cheshire, 1982; Thorne & Henley, 1975; Trudgill, 1974). Not only is it possible to detect linguistic differences between male and female speech in global terms, but variables such as whether participants are in single sex or mixed groups can be shown to have an effect on language production. A good deal of the work on the language and lives of young blacks in Britain and elsewhere has had a very strong male bias, both in terms of the investigators and the subjects selected for investigation (cf. Fuller, 1983; Spender, 1980). It was therefore felt to be particularly important that male and female speakers should be represented in approximately equal numbers in the sample, and a total of 21 young women and 24 young men took part in recordings.

It was also felt preferable to arrange single sex groups of speakers and investigators wherever possible to avoid any variation which might be attributable to inhibiting factors inherent in mixed sex conversation. This is clearly of great importance in informal black conversation. The pilot study for the project had employed just one black female fieldworker who had experienced greater difficulty in eliciting casual speech from male than female subjects. For this reason it was felt essential to use both male and female fieldworkers for the main study.

Social networks

We have already discussed the problematic nature of a social class analysis for the British Black community (see Sampling Methodology above). Linguists such as Gal (1979) and Milroy (1980), however, have proposed network relations as an extremely valuable alternative to social class in sociolinguistic analysis. Unlike class it is independent of intercultural differences in economic or status systems, and can be applied without difficulty to a wide range of communities.

Essentially, social network measures a person's degree of group membership. Relations with other people can be of two main kinds: open and closed. In closed networks there is more contact with other members of the same network than with those outside. Such networks are dense; they are also multiplex inasmuch as individuals will often interact with each other in a number of roles, such as kin, neighbour and fellow employee. Understandably, membership of a closed network will be associated with strong pressure to observe the behavioural norms of the group. Open networks, in contrast, are characterized by low density relations in which individual contacts will not necessarily know each other. People are usually related to each other in only one capacity and far less social pressure can be exerted over individuals' behaviour.

Personal relations in rural communities (cf. Gal, 1979) and working class communities in old established areas of cities (cf. Young & Wilmott, 1962) tend to be dense and multiplex. Studies of West Indian societies (cf. W. Edwards, 1984), and black urban communities in Britain (cf. Pryce, 1979) and America (cf. Hannerz, 1974) reflect the same pattern. The precise determinants of the kinds of network relations will vary from community to community. In Gal's (1979) study of Austrian–Hungarian bilinguals, degrees of peasantness proved to be critical; in W. Edwards (1984) study of urban and rural communities in Guyana vernacular urban culture was marked by frequenting of rum shops, street dancing and preference for certain kinds of music and dress, while vernacular rural culture was associated with attendance at certain African-derived pre-nuptial festivities, rustic dress and Afro-Guyanese cuisine. Close ethnographic observation is therefore necessary to enable the analyst to identify the important factors for a given community.

In the context of the present study, it was felt to be important to find out as much as possible about the patterns of work, friendship and leisure of subjects included in the sample. For instance, the network relations of young people who lived in a predominantly black neighbourhood, attended their parents' Pentecostal Church and based their social life entirely upon the Church would be more dense and multiplex than those of young people living in a predominantly black area, but working mainly with white people and socializing in racially mixed groups. Previous knowledge of the speakers was supplemented with information which they volunteered in the course of recordings and in answer to direct questions, to ensure that the information gathered was as full as possible.

Employment proved to be a very important indicator of social network. In just one case, a participant was employed in a factory where a large proportion of the workforce was known to be black. The majority of those in employment, however, indicated that there were very few black people or that they were the only black person in that particular place of work. In contrast, those young people who were unemployed — some 50% of the young women and 58% of the young men — would clearly spend their time in the company of other unemployed friends. Since all the speakers indicated that two or more of their best friends were black, it is reasonable to assume that the social networks of young unemployed people would be more black than those of young people who were in employment and in daily contact with whites.

It is interesting to compare the effect of employment on network in the present study with the situation reported by the Milroys for Belfast. Of the three communities studied, East Belfast, Shankhill and the Falls, only East Belfast had a low rate of unemployment and most of the male participants were connected in one capacity or another with the shipyard. Both the Shankhill and the Falls, however, had high rates of unemployment and those men in employment worked in a wide range of places, often considerable distances from home. The effect of employment in East Belfast was the formation of social networks which were often extremely dense and multiplex. The employment situation in Dudley, however, is closer to that of Shankhill and the Falls. The minority position of black workers in a predominantly white society ensures that work more often isolates individuals from their ethnic roots rather than consolidating their position within it, particularly in view of the very high rate of unemployment in the black community. The pattern which emerges would appear to be the consequence of close-knit relationships never having been organized round the workplace, but rather associated with unemployed groups.

Another important factor in determining social networks is place of residence. Most of the black population of Dudley is concentrated in a long, narrow area which extends outwards from the city centre, and some 75% of the young people lived in this area. However, nine people came from an area known as the Wren's Nest. This is an almost exclusively white council estate. Speakers who live in this area attended the neighbourhood secondary school which also drew on a very small proportion of black pupils. The experience of young black people living in this area is necessarily very different from those living in areas of high ethnic minority concentration.

Network scores which measured the degree of integration of speakers into the black community were calculated for all the speakers. These scores were based on answers to a wide range of questions. Speakers were asked where they lived and whether they were employed. They were also asked to name their three closest friends, and to indicate whether they were black or white and where they went together (for instance, youth club, work, Church or sport). Thus, if speakers went to more than one place with a given friend, it suggested that network relations were multiplex and, if they went to the same place with more than one friend, that relations were dense. They were also asked questions about their leisure activities. Attention was paid to whether speakers mentioned known black activities, such as Pentecostal Church or the local black youth club. Level of involvement was also noted.

Thus if a speaker was a committed Christian rather than an occasional Church-goer they would be involved in a wide range of extra activities such as Bible Class and Church youth club; or if they were voluntary youth leaders they would be very regular and not casual attenders at the club. Finally, questions were asked about whether speakers saw white friends and neighbours socially often, sometimes or never.

TABLE 1 *Calculation of Network Scores*

	Range
Employment	0 to 1
Residence	0 to 1
Black friends	0 to 3
Activities with black friends: dense	0 to 1
multiplex	0 to 1
Social activities	0 to 2
White friends	— 1 to 1
White neighbours	— 1 to 1
Total	— 2 to 11

Actual scores ranged from 2 to 10. Figure 1 (on page 60) shows that the spread between the two extremes was good, but that males and females tended to pattern differently, males being more likely to have a higher network score than females.

Education

Subjects' level of education is another variable which is sometimes considered in sociolinguistic studies (cf. Jahangiri & Hudson, 1982), and which also proves to be problematic in the context of the British Black community. The level of underachievement in schools of children of West Indian descent has received a great deal of discussion in the last ten years. Black children have been over-represented in low streams, non-exam classes and schools for the educationally sub-normal; they have been under-represented in selective schools, upper streams and exam classes and in further and higher education (Rampton, 1981; Tomlinson, 1980). Educational aspirations, in contrast, on the part of both parents and children, have always tended to be high (Black People's Progressive Association, 1978). It is therefore more realistic to consider not only actual educational achievement but also plans for the future. Subjects selected for the study ranged from former pupils of schools for the educationally subnormal to polytechnic students; they also included some young people with no plans to do further exams or vocational training; some who were part-time students in

FIGURE 1 *Distribution of Network Scores for Male and Female Speakers*

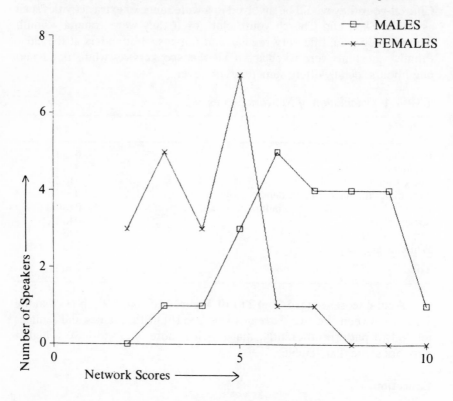

O and A level classes; and some who were full-time students on Access courses, which may enable them to pursue higher education although they do not fulfil the formal entry requirements.

Education was measured on a scale from 0–10. Points were awarded for examination successes already achieved, and for planned courses of study and further training.

TABLE 2 *Calculation of Education Scores*

CSEs	passed: 2	planned: 1
O-levels	passed: 4	planned: 2
A-levels	passed: 6	planned: 3
Craft training (e.g. City and Guilds)		1
Professional training (e.g. State Registered Nurse)		2
Tertiary Education (including "Access")		3

Scores varied between 0 and 10, as we can see in Figure 2 below which shows the distribution of education scores for male and female speakers.

FIGURE 2 *Distribution of Education Scores for Male and Female Speakers*

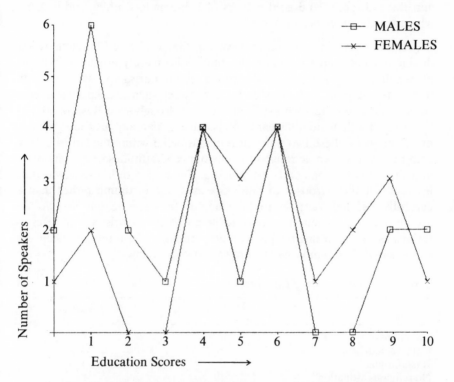

Again we find a good spread of scores, but with a slight imbalance between males and females, the females tending to perform and aspire higher than the males. The pattern reflects trends reported in the population at large for black children which have been discussed in Chapter 2.

Acquiescence–criticalness

A number of writers have chosen to describe the differing responses of young black people to the realities of racial inequality in terms of typologies of life styles. It is not difficult to understand why observers have found this approach attractive. There are, for instance, various groups which can be clearly defined by both physical appearance and behaviour. One such group is the large black Pentecostal Christian community. Although there is variation between congregations, both men and women are expected to dress modestly and conservatively. Behaviour, too, is regulated by the group and young people's social lives are restricted in the main to Church activities. Another such group are the Rastafarians. They can be recognized by their dread locks, which symbolize the rejection of black people's inferior status and the red, green and gold colours of Ethiopia in clothing and badges, which signify allegiance to Africa.

It is important to remember, however, that within the Church there is a distinction between Christians and those who merely attend, usually to please their parents. Some of the young men in our sample said that they wore their hair in locks out of fashion rather than a deep Rastafarian conviction, and others who sympathize very strongly with Rastafarian beliefs said that they did not wear locks because of parental pressure. What is more, between these two poles of religious belief within the British Black community lies a whole range of behaviours and attitudes which cannot — and should not — be neatly categorized. The notion of life style was thus invoked for the purposes of fieldwork as a rule of thumb rather than a carefully defined variable to be studied. In selecting our sample we attempted to make sure that reasonable numbers of Christians and Rastafarians as well as young people with no particular religious allegiance were represented. The sample can be broken down as follows:

TABLE 3 *Distribution of Life Styles*

	Males	Females
Christians	6	6
Churchgoers	6	4
Rastafarians	5	1
No religious affiliation	9	8

The main imbalance in the sample was between the numbers of male and female Rastafarians. There is some evidence that the appeal of Rastafarianism would seem to be much higher for young men than it is for young women. Fuller (1980), for instance, notes that in her observation of young people in a London secondary school some of the males but none of the females displayed the externalia of Rastafarianism by the fifth year. She concludes from interviews with the young people that a Rasta identity was more difficult for females to contemplate. It is therefore not at all surprising that we found it extremely difficult to locate female Rastafarians.

It should also be remembered that lifestyle is partly subsumed under the notion of social network, discussed above. Christians are likely to have very dense and multiplex networks, as too are Rastafarians, whereas those who do not subscribe to a particular named lifestyle are likely to have a more diffuse and open-ended network system. The main differences between Christians and Rastafarians, on the other hand, probably lie in their attitudes towards mainstream white society, inasmuch as Christians may tend to be more accepting and conformist. Following on the work of Fuller (1983), therefore, a scale of acquiescence/criticalness was devised, based on speakers' opinions of school, work and the police, as expressed both in discussion and in response to the following questions:

— How would you describe your time at school?
   Very happy/quite happy/OK/quite unhappy/very unhappy

— How many teachers do you think were prejudiced against black children?
   All or almost all/more than half/about half/less than half/none or very few

— What about white people as a whole?
   All or almost all/more than half/about half/less than half/none or very few

— How do you think teachers found *you* as a person?
   Very co-operative/quite co-operative/OK/quite difficult/very difficult

— How do you think teachers found the way you worked?
   Very hardworking/quite hardworking/OK/quite lazy/very lazy

— What do you think of the way the police treat black people?
   Very fair/quite fair/OK/quite unfair/very unfair

— If you were stopped and questioned by the police what would you do?
   Try to get away/co-operate but complain/co-operate without complaining

Potential scores on this measure ranged from $+13$ to -13. Actual scores varied between $+7$ and -7. Such a scale has the advantage of being able to accommodate the full range of opinions and does not depend on predetermined categories. The two measures — social network and views towards mainstream white society — were felt to be a more reliable means of differentiating subjects than membership of some externally defined life style, because they recognize the diversity which exists within the black community in a way which eludes any attempt at a life style analysis.

FIGURE 3 *Distribution of Acquiescence–Criticalness Scores for Male and Female Speakers*

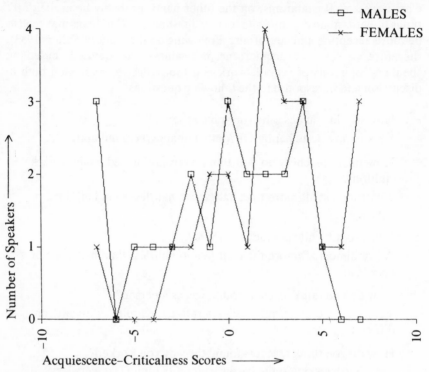

In this case male and female speakers achieve the same range of scores though, overall, males tend to be more critical than females.

Adequacy of the sample

Some conditions were easier to satisfy than others in locating subjects. It was a simple matter to approach Christian subjects through Church networks and to identify Rastafarians by their appearance. It was also fairly straightforward to ensure that there were equal numbers of males and females, that subjects' parents came from Jamaica and that they themselves had been born in Britain and had lived all their lives in Dudley. Only three subjects presented problems in this respect. On two occasions, the black fieldworker was very surprised to discover towards the end of recording that one member of the group was in fact of mixed race. In both the cases, the young people's perception of themselves as black, together with their acceptance as members of black friendship groups, made it seem reasonable to include them in the sample. On another occasion it emerged that one of the speakers had come to Britain from Jamiaca at the age of six. Since there were no very obvious differences in the linguistic behaviour of this young man and the rest of the sample, it was decided to include him in the analysis unless closer examination of his speech showed him to be in any way anomalous.

Various other characteristics could not be determined in advance. For instance, it was only possible to discover attitudes towards mainstream white society, social networks and educational aspirations by fairly detailed questioning during the course of the actual recording. As it transpired, the sample was remarkable for the excellent spread of scores for these variables. It was less impressive when each of these variables was broken down into male and female components. Although the numbers of males and females were approximately equal (males: 24; females: 21) the distribution of scores tended to differ between the sexes, so that males as a group were more critical, had more exclusively black social networks and had lower educational scores. In each of these cases the patterns observed accorded with independent observations on young black people (see, for instance, Chapter 2) and it is not at all surprising that these trends should be repeated in the sample. However, it is important to note that, although analysis would have been simpler if girls' scores had covered a range in all cases identical with that of the boys, the range of scores for both sexes was nonetheless sufficiently comparable to make further analysis perfectly feasible.

Summary

The present study is based on some 45 young British-born black people of Jamaican parents. They are aged between 16 and 23 and live in Dudley, West Midlands. It is impossible to obtain a random sample of British Black speakers because of their skewed distribution in both social and geographical terms, and because of the absence of ready made sample frames. Instead, it was decided to work with a "judgement" sample, which identifies the types of speaker of interest for the study, and seeks out a quota of people who meet the various requirements. The characteristics identified as potentially interesting for a study of the social influences on British Black language use included the speakers' sex, their social network relations, their educational achievements and aspirations, and their attitudes towards mainstream white society.

6 Data collection in a British Black community

In the previous chapter we considered questions pertaining to sampling methodology and the composition of the group of young people who took part in recording. In order to clarify the relationship between research objectives and research design, we need to extend the discussion from the sampling of speakers to the sampling of language. A socially sensitive account of British Black language must be based on the speech produced by a wide range of speakers. However, it must also take into consideration the situational constraints on these speakers and the extent of individual and community linguistic repertoires.

The collection of speech data raises a very wide range of issues for the researcher. The aim of the present chapter is to provide a framework for the discussion of the particular problems associated with the British Black community. A number of pressing questions need to be considered and resolved before it is possible to proceed. For example, which speech style (or styles) should form the focus for description? Can fieldwork be undertaken by a skilled and sensitive outsider or is it imperative to enlist the services of an "inside" fieldworker? Each of these questions will be considered in turn, before describing the fieldwork techniques adopted in the present study.

Which speech style?

Traditional dialectology draws on the speech of older, rural males who have never moved from their place of birth. The rationale for this choice has been that this is the group which retain the most conservative speech patterns (cf. Orton *et al.*, 1962: 15), and therefore forms the most appropriate starting point for studies of linguistic change. The major challenge to dialectology came only in the 1960s with the work of William Labov. Although Labov shared the keen interest of dialectologists in linguistic change, he made extremely important innovations in methodology which have allowed the study of language in its social context to develop in many exciting new directions.

His early work on the dialect of Martha's Vineyard (Labov, 1963) drew on conversational data from a wide range of islanders, as well as reading passages and word lists. He also gathered a great deal of background information on speakers. This approach allowed him to note the regularity, the direction and, most important, the social motivation for sound changes. Significantly, his findings challenged the notion that the most reliable speakers of the vernacular were older people by showing that the heaviest users of the pronunciation of the /ay/ and /aw/ diphthongs normally associated with conservative speakers in Martha's Vineyard were in fact the young, sometimes highly educated men, who had deliberately chosen to stay on the island rather than to seek work on the mainland. Threatened by the presence on the island of wealthy summer visitors and their very different life style and values, these young men were defining a separate local identity for themselves which was clearly mirrored in distinct language patterns.

One of the most obvious implications of the Martha's Vineyard study was that the focus of study should be extended well beyond that of older male speakers. It also became clear that if linguists were to be able to interpret their data, information on the social background of speakers needed to be collected. Labov first put these principles into operation in his highly innovative and influential study of the speech of Lower East Side New Yorkers (Labov, 1966), which drew on individual speakers using speech of varying degrees of formality. The formal speech of the interview was supplemented with three kinds of reading style (continuous prose, word lists and minimal pairs). Casual speech was obtained by asking speakers to recount any life endangering events which they may have experienced, or by including speech which took place when another member of the household entered the room.

The fieldwork techniques in the early Labov work undoubtedly allowed access to more formal speech styles but various writers have noted shortcomings in the elicitation of casual speech. Macaulay's (1977) study of Glasgow and Shuy, Wolfram & Riley's (1968) account of Detroit speech, both drawing on the Labovian framework, document only one fairly formal conversational style. Gal (1979) notes that early attempts at interviews with Austrian informants produced a frustratingly narrow range of styles, despite efforts to encourage involvement and informality. Sutcliffe (1982a) makes similar observations for British Black speakers. This raises two important questions: first, can data based only on more formal speech styles constitute a sufficient basis for analysis?; second, is there any way in which one speech style is of greater interest to the linguist than another?

There is little doubt that the answer to the first question must be in the negative. Various writers have in fact questioned the adequacy of a database which fails to tap the most informal styles for an accurate analysis of the speech of a given community. Douglas-Cowie (1978), for instance, has demonstrated the limitations on data which can be imposed by formality. In her investigation of the Ulster Scots dialect spoken in the village of Articlave, she recorded both in-group talk with friends and neighbours and then conversation alone with an English outsider. The presence of the outsider provoked a clearly discernible move to more standard speech. Sufficient data for the analysis of the local dialect was only to be found in the in-group records. Milroy (1980) notes that the accurate description of the [ʌ] variant in Belfast would almost certainly have been impossible if the study had been confined to more formal varieties.

The answer to the question as to whether some speech styles are of greater interest to the linguist than others has had varying responses. Again Labov has been highly influential in guiding thought. His earlier work (Labov, 1966) focuses on more formal speech styles, but various ideas developed during the course of the New York study led him to place greater emphasis subsequently on casual speech. He claims, for instance, that casual styles are characterized by less careful audio-monitoring and are less subject to conscious control. For this reason they provide the most systematic data for the analysis of linguistic structure, against which more formal styles can be calibrated. Thus, in his later work, he changes the emphasis from large scale representative studies of entire communities which sample a wide range of speech styles to smaller scale group studies which look in some considerable depth at the most casual style, which he characterizes as the vernacular.

This interest in the vernacular is reflected in a wide range of studies, including Cheshire's (1982) description of the language of adolescents in Reading and Milroy's (1980) discussion of language in working class Belfast communities. But, while the importance of vernacular speech is recognized by most writers, not all accept uncritically Labov's contention that informal relaxed speech receives least careful audio-monitoring. Wolfson (1976), for instance, illustrates how some speakers can be at their most self-conscious when trying to produce informal speech. Gal (1979) provides examples of informants who, contrary to the predictions of the audio-monitoring model, did not vary their speech in any significant way even when engaged in emotion-laden personal narrative. She suggests that the audio-monitoring view neglects the symbolic and expressive uses of language, and argues that any style of speech which is felt by speakers to be appropriate to a situation must be considered natural:

"The focus on studying casual speech results in the neglect of communicative skills that enable the speaker to pick the variety appropriate to the social context, whether or not the context is formal. In the search for the most natural style, speakers' many communicative abilities appear as obstacles to be circumvented rather than as subjects of investigation."

In the context of the present study it was felt essential to explore the full range of speakers' speech styles. The vernacular is of special interest inasmuch as it is often the least accessible to the "outside observer". It is also the part of the speakers' linguistic repertoire which is most likely to have undergone innovation and change in a British context and therefore possibly offers the greatest challenge to both the sociolinguist and the descriptive linguist. However, a description which focussed exclusively on the vernacular aspects of British Black speech would give a very incomplete picture of both community and individual repertoires. The need for a broader approach may also be related to the nature of the linguistic situation under study. The British Black community, which would seem to be undergoing a process of language shift, may well have more in common with the bilingual Oberwart community described by Gal than with the more stable communities which form the focus for studies such as Labov *et al.* (1968) and Cheshire (1982).

"Insider" versus "outsider" approaches

The decision to sample the total range of community and individual repertoires has far-reaching implications for the decision as to who actually undertakes the fieldwork. Labov *et al.* (1968) made an important methodological innovation by combining the insights of professional linguists with the "inside" knowledge of Black American language and culture of non-linguist fieldworkers. Whereas Shuy *et al.*'s (1968) study of Detroit Negro speech elicited only fairly formal speech styles, Labov *et al.*'s Harlem project succeeded in recording truly informal "vernacular" speech, and what the study lost in representativeness it gained in depth. It should be noted, too, that the fieldwork techniques employed in the Harlem study moved a great distance from the interview format which had characterized much earlier work. Fieldworkers were careful to create very relaxed and spontaneous peer group situations, in which the presence of the group was sufficiently strong to override the possibly inhibiting effect of the tape recorder.

The problem of what Labov has termed "the observer's paradox" has subsequently been approached in a number of ways, all drawing in various ways on notions of reciprocal relations. Gal's method of data collection, for instance, is in the classic anthropological tradition and is based on full participation in the life of the Oberwart community, with its attendant rights and obligations, over a period of a year. Few other sociolinguists have been able to devote as much time to their fieldwork. Cheshire's study of Reading working class adolescents, for instance, was based on some 20 hours of conversation recorded on visits to adventure playgrounds over a period of several months. Her acceptance by the young people was dependent to some extent on her novelty value as a woman arriving on a motor bike. But her success in recording vernacular speech must have derived in large part from the sympathetic interest and friendship which she showed to them as individuals. Milroy (1980) gained access to Belfast vernacular speech by exploiting network relations and introducing herself as a "friend of a friend". In return for the opportunity to spend time in people's homes recording their conversation, she offered favours such as the use of her van and she also participated in community life in various ways.

In some situations, however, structural constraints, such as the sex or ethnicity of the investigator, will make it impossible to achieve acceptance by all or even most members of the group. It is certainly possible to obtain authentic vernacular speech in inter-racial situations (cf. Sutcliffe, 1982a), but a great deal of time, effort and sensitivity needs to be spent in "establishing credentials". Further, the fact that only a small proportion of speakers can be counted upon to produce what is essentially a vernacular "performance" in an extremely unnatural speech situation makes it difficult to generalize from these speakers to the community as a whole. The picture which emerges from interracial or even intersexual fieldwork techniques is thus inevitably partial, and, in order to ensure that the data base faithfully reflects authentic language behaviour in a wide range of situations, it is essential to use an "insider".

However, racial identity is not sufficient in itself to ensure access to vernacular speech. Milroy (personal communication), for instance, found that a young man who recorded conversation from friends and neighbours in Ballymacarrett obtained highly stilted, formal speech. Le Page (1972) speculates that the Spanish influenced children in the Belize study may have reacted unfavourably to the Jamaican fieldworker. The same problem was encountered in the pilot for the present study. It had been assumed that the presence of a sympathetic young black fieldworker recording relaxed conversation would ensure Patois usage, but this did not prove to be the case. Clearly, the black fieldworker has a considerable advantage over the white fieldworker in this situation, but successful recording of vernacular speech requires the establishment of genuine social relationships and the creation of realistic speech situations, irrespective of racial identity. It became clear that the use of both "inside" and "outside" fieldworkers who would elicit a wide range of speech styles was essential, but that it was also necessary to develop other techniques which would ensure that the most vernacular speech was represented in the data base.

Careful ethnographic observation of interaction in the British Black community is clearly a prerequisite for study. It is essential, for instance, that the fieldworker should have credibility with participants, so that if they do not already know each other they should at least be able to claim "friend of a friend" status (cf. Milroy, 1980). Having established their credentials, it is important to be able to offer something in return. For some young people, the opportunity to express their views on matters of some personal importance would have been enough; others, particularly those who had no strong ties of friendship with the fieldworkers, required something more since they clearly perceived the invitation to take part in recording to be an unacceptably one-sided arrangement. Following the many precedents to be found in the sociological and psychological literature, it was decided to offer participants an interview fee. The acceptance of a fee signalled an acknowledgement that there should be fair exchange between the different parties.

This arrangement ensured co-operation for the recording of "public" speech, but a good deal of careful thought was necessary to encourage participants to use Patois speech. Our observation made it clear that many young black people use Patois only in in-group conversation, so that the presence of any other person, even the young black fieldworker, would be enough to inhibit Patois usage. The obvious solution was to create a situation in which the young people were left alone. They were given a questionnaire and asked to discuss the answers among themselves before completing it. Many of the questions were about black language and culture and the treatment of black people by the dominant white society, all topics which in our experience trigger a switch to Patois.

Data collection: Implications for the present study

Considerable confusion surrounds patterns of language use among British born blacks in the minds of many white people. It has passed into conventional wisdom that Patois is used regularly by only a very small proportion of young people, and that those who do take pride in "talking black" are associated with aspects of black youth culture such as reggae and Rastafarianism. In order to explore these assumptions and to construct a fuller picture of the extent and determinants of Patois usage it is obviously important to sample the entire linguistic repertoire of a group of speakers.

There has been a great deal of emphasis in recent years on the vernacular as the most authentic speech against which other varieties can be calibrated (cf. Labov, 1972; Cheshire, 1982). The central role of the vernacular in our understanding of the language usage of British born black people is clearly of considerable interest and the reliance on self-reports rather than direct observation of Patois usage in many previous studies represents a serious weakness in methodology. But it must also be remembered that there are indications that, for at least some of these young people, a diglossic situation prevails in which English is more characteristic of formal "public" situations and mixed Patois and English in informal "private" situations. A description which focussed only on the vernacular would thus be just as partial as one which was restricted to more formal speech.

In order to sample the entire linguistic repertoire of a speaker, it is necessary to make use of both "inside" and "outside" fieldworkers. The status of insider, however, has to be earned. Under normal circumstances this involves a considerable investment of time, which when translated into research funding represents a very large financial underwriting. Although, in the context of the present study, it is not enough to be young and black to be accepted as an insider, close ethnographic observation provides a clear picture of the circumstances which tend to give rise to Patois usage. Any research design which incorporates this information is likely to be able to tap the kind of language used in a range of carefully and appropriately selected situations.

Fieldwork procedures

Some 45 young black people who fulfilled the conditions described above were located through the network relations of the two black fieldworkers on the project, Leighton Bruce and Carol Tomlin. The pilot study had demonstrated the success of this approach for primary social contacts and also the majority of young people who had been contacted by the fieldworkers in the role of "friend of a friend" (cf. Milroy, 1980). However, a small number of second order contacts, predominantly Rastafarian males, were extremely suspicious of the motives for recording and were unwilling to take part. Resources were not available to finance a protracted period of fieldwork. It was therefore not possible in all cases for fieldworkers to establish their "credentials" or build trusting relationships with all potential speakers. An essential feature of such relationships is reciprocity and the offering of favours which in turn create obligations. It was felt, however, that the condition of reciprocity could be satisfied by paying speakers an interview fee, a practice more common in sociological surveys than in sociolinguistic fieldwork. Friends and friends of friends expressed surprise and willingness to forego the interview fee, but those who fell outside the network relations of the fieldworkers, primarily Rastafarians, found this arrangement acceptable.

Subjects were seen in single-sexed friendship groups of two or three in Leighton Bruce's flat. This is situated in a council-owned tower block in an area of Dudley with high black settlement. They were told that Leighton, Carol and the white interviewer, David Sutcliffe, were working on an ESRC funded project designed to find out more about British-born black people, though no specific reference was made to language. This position was taken for a number of reasons. First, speakers' reports of their own language tend to be extremely unreliable (cf. Labov, 1966). Secondly, because black language tends to have very low status, the most likely effect of telling participants that language is the main focus of the study would be to cause embarrassment and to give rise to misleading responses (see Chapter 3 for further discussion). Finally, our interest in issues relating to socio-political aspects of life in Britain for black people was genuine and not simply convenient. It was a basic assumption of the project that the language use of British Black people could be understood only within its social context.

Firm assurances were made about the confidentiality of the interviews, particularly in the case of speakers known to the black fieldworkers, whose primary concern was often that their conversation would not be reported to their parents. They were also introduced to a fourth person, Jeremy Green. It was explained that he was not officially part of the project, but was simply looking after the tape recorder.

Both the casette deck and the microphones were placed as inconspicuously as possible, but no attempt was made to conceal the fact that the interviews were being recorded, for obvious ethical reasons. There were also practical considerations. Fieldwork for both the pilot and the main study was done during the summer. The quality of the recording for the pilot study was seriously impaired by traffic noise and it was obvious that windows would have to be closed when recording was taking place for the main study. Since the temperature was in the eighties, an explanation of why it was important not to open the windows had to be given. No attempt was made to deliberately mislead those taking part, but most people automatically assumed that the recording was limited to the formal parts of the session and quickly forgot about the presence of the tape recorder.

Interview sequence

We were particularly interested in the effects of ethnicity and formality on language use and so constructed interviews in a way which would allow us to control for these variables. Most of the recordings began with David Sutcliffe, a white researcher, asking a series of questions to do in the main with education. The situation was defined as formal by the age difference between interviewer and interviewees, by the interviewer's fairly formal style of dress and manner, and by the fact that the other people present deliberately referred to him as Mr Sutcliffe. In about a third of the recordings, this interview was left until last so as to ensure that any differences which emerged in language use could be attributed to the formal white situation rather than any kind of "warming up" effect.

After about 20 minutes, Carol Tomlin took over in the case of female speakers and Leighton Bruce in the case of male speakers, as a previous pilot had demonstrated that it was extremely difficult to elicit a full range of speech in mixed sex conversation. The first encounter with the black fieldworkers continued the interview format and was designed to be a formal one. Participants were asked questions on interest and leisure pursuits which the fieldworker read off a printed form and answers were written down, before moving on to more open ended discussion of matters of concern to the black community, such as relations with the police and media coverage. At the end of these formal interviews, the fieldworkers left the room, explaining that they had to find and staple together some questionnaires which they wanted the speakers to answer, and that they would be back shortly.

The young people were then left in the room with Jeremy, a 20-year-old white student who also comes from the West Midlands. The situation was defined as informal by the nearness in age of the participants, the casual dress and manner of Jeremy who spent the duration of the recording sitting on the floor, and the fact that he dissociated himself from the preceding interviews. He explained that he was not a part of the main research team but had been interested in some of the things they had been discussing. The conversation which followed was thus informal and ethnically mixed.

When the black fieldworker returned with the questionnaires, speakers were invited to discuss the various questions among themselves, before completing the forms. It was explained that they would be left completely alone because no one wanted to influence their answers. Areas which they were asked to consider included their attitudes to mainstream white society and their own network relations. Since it was not always possible to discuss these matters directly and in detail with the young people, this provided useful information on background variables which could later be correlated with linguistic variables. Questions were also asked about areas which, in our experience, regularly provoke a switch to Patois. These areas include direct discussion of proverbs and other Patois usage and treatment of black people by the police. In this way some 23 hours of conversation were recorded from 17 different groups of speakers.

FIGURE 4 *Recording Sequence*

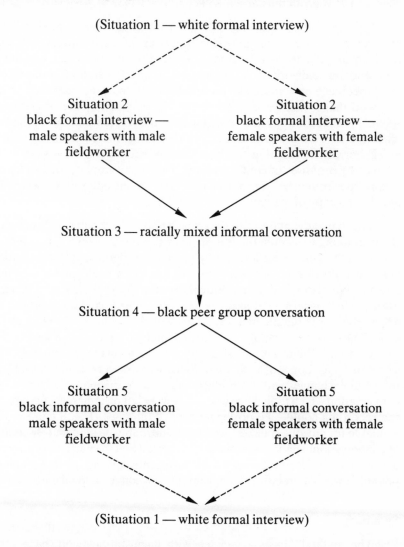

(Situation 1 — white formal interview)

Situation 2
black formal interview —
male speakers with male
fieldworker

Situation 2
black formal interview —
female speakers with female
fieldworker

Situation 3 — racially mixed informal conversation

Situation 4 — black peer group conversation

Situation 5
black informal conversation
male speakers with male
fieldworker

Situation 5
black informal conversation
female speakers with female
fieldworker

(Situation 1 — white formal interview)

The success of this format was evident from the outset. The interviews with both black and white fieldworkers were clearly perceived as formal, with speakers adhering fairly strictly to turn-taking, and offering information only to those questions posed by the interviewer. There was a visible relaxation at the end of the interviews and conversation first with Jeremy and later with the black fieldworker over biscuits and drinks was marked by longer utterances, a greater number of interruptions and more equal exchanges between all the participants.

Most gratifying, however, was the success of leaving speakers alone after an initial "warm-up" period in triggering informal conversation. Subjects which were discussed included boyfriends and girlfriends, new underwear and the fieldworkers. The frankness of the discussion left no doubt that most people had completely forgotten about the tape recorder or had assumed that it had been switched off. On a small number of occasions, speakers realized they were being taped in the last few minutes of the time allocated for peer group conversation. One group ran out from the room in mock horror, threatening to "beat Jeremy batty", but were suitably reassured by promises of confidentiality. Two other groups provided special Patois "performances" for our benefit, and on one occasion we were even asked for a copy of the tape.

The main advantage of this approach to fieldwork was purely practical. By attempting to sample the full range of the young people's speech in the course of the same recording, we by-passed considerable problems in locating and following up speakers who all too often could prove extremely elusive. We also avoided the difficulties of creating situations sufficiently informal for triggering Patois usage and were able to standardize procedures across the whole sample in a way which would have been otherwise impossible. The only disadvantage was the unavoidable limitation on the length of the recording. We felt it unrealistic to ask informants to give up more than one-and-a-half hours of their time. Since we wished to sample formal and informal exchanges with both black and white participants, as well as the conversation which took place when they were left on their own, each part of the recording could take no longer than 20 minutes. The amount of data available for any one speaker would thus inevitably be limited. Observation of conversational patterns, however, suggested that the patterns of language use which would emerge would be sufficiently distinct to make analysis possible even with relatively small amounts of conversational data.

Summary

The methodologists associated with linguistic fieldwork have varied enormously over the years and are still very much in a state of evolution. A wide range of issues of importance for linguistic fieldwork were discussed. For instance, the question of which speech style should be studied, and whether any one style is of particular interest to the linguist was considered. In terms of the present study, it was decided that it was essential to sample as wide a range as practicable of speakers' linguistic repertoires. In order to achieve this end, another question needed careful consideration: should investigators be "insiders" in the community, "outsiders" or a mixture of the two? Given that the aim was to record a wide range of speech, a decision was made to use both inside and outside fieldworkers. Reservations were expressed, however, about the ability of even inside fieldworkers to consistently elicit vernacular speech in a British Black context. For this reason, all outside constraints were removed and a situation was created where participants were recorded on their own, discussing a questionnaire which contains subjects known to provoke Patois usage.

7 A quantitative analysis of the data

In order to adequately describe the full complexities of the patterns which emerge from the data and their relationship with social variables, it is necessary to construct a variety of linguistic measures. The starting point for this description will be the frequency with which Patois variants are used both within each situation and over recording as a whole. The construction of a Patois index based on some 11 frequently occurring features will be described and the effects of both situational constraints and of ethnicity on this index will be considered in some detail. It will be argued that an overall score of Patois frequency, derived from the mean index scores for each speaker, forms the best basis for correlations with other sociological variables described in Chapter 5. The effects of attitudes towards mainstream white society, the interaction of sex and education and the social networks of the speakers on Patois frequency will be assessed. Finally, three case studies are offered to illustrate the trends abstracted in the quantitative analysis, and to point to other directions in which the study of British Black language can be developed.

The construction of a Patois index

Preliminary analysis indicated remarkable consistency in patterning for a very wide range of Patois variants. It was felt preferable to attempt correlations between social variables and language using a Patois index, a single measure made up of frequency scores across a large number of variants, rather than a smaller number of individual variants. This decision was based partly on the uniformity of direction in the choice of English and Patois variants. However, such an approach also has the advantage of overcoming the problems of empty cells caused by insufficient data (cf. Le Page, 1975) by allowing the analyst to work with the mean score. This course of action would be inappropriate if Patois variants patterned differently, but seems acceptable in view of the fact that they vary along the same dimension in response to the same social constraints.

The calculation of scores

The fieldwork was designed to control as carefully as possible certain situational variables which have been observed to affect the language behaviour of young black people. The most important of these are formality and the ethnicity of the participants. Young black people were recorded in some five different situations: in a formal interview with a white researcher (situation 1); in a formal interview with a black researcher (situation 2); in informal racially mixed conversation (situation 3); in informal peer group conversation without the presence of a researcher (situation 4); and in informal conversation with a black researcher (situation 5). The ordering of the different parts of the recording was carefully controlled in order to maximize the effects of formality; so, too, were the personal characteristics and behaviour of the researchers.

The first question of concern was therefore the variation which might exist both between situations and between individual speakers' treatment of the different situations. Frequencies were calculated for each variant in the standard way:

$$\frac{\text{No. of tokens of Patois Variant}}{\text{No. of tokens of Patois and English variants}} \times 100$$

A score of 100 would thus indicate completely English usage and a score of 0 completely Patois usage. In practice, because Patois was usually used in conjunction with English as a part of code switching behaviour, most scores were considerably nearer to 100 than they were to 0. Using the frequency scores for individual variants, a *Patois Index* was then constructed which was based on the mean scores of speakers on 11 frequently occurring linguistic variables for each of the situations.

When the index scores for individual speakers in all five situations are closely examined, a number of striking features emerge. First, the lowest index score, indicating most Patois usage, is located for all subjects in either situation 4, where participants were left alone, or situation 5, where they chatted informally with the black fieldworker. For all but seven subjects, highest Patois usage was found when the young people were left on their own. Two of these speakers (31 and 36) had very similar scores for situations

TABLE 4 *Linguistic Variables in the Patois Index*

---

1. *Dentals*
   English variants: /θ,ð/, e.g. /θin, ðen/ — thin, then
   Patois variants: /t, d/, e.g. /tik, dat/ — thick, that
2. *Vowels*
   English variants: /ʌ/ (Received Pronunciation), /ʊ/ (West Midlands), e.g. /rʌn/, /rʊn/ — run
   Patois variant: /o/, e.g. /fon/ — fun
3. *Third person singular present tense verbs*
   English variant: John *swims* fast; Kevin *eats* a lot
   Patois variant: John *swim* fast; Kevin *eat* a lot
4. *Plurals*
   English variant: six *cars*; all the *books*
   Patois variant: six *car*; all di *book*
5. *Simple past tense*
   English variants: Winston *saw* the boy; Beverley *walked* away
   Patois variant: Winston *see* di boy; Beverley *walk* away
6. *Copulas* (before adjectives and verbs)
   English variants: The man *is* happy; John *is* coming
   Patois variants: Di man *happy*; John *a come*
7. *First person singular pronoun*
   English variant: *I* feel happy
   Patois variant: *me* feel happy
8. *Third person singular pronouns*
   English variant: *he* put it away
   Patois variant: *im* put it away
9. *Third person plural pronouns*
   English variants: *they* like the baby; look at *their* hats
   Patois variant: *dem* like di baby; look at *dem* hat
10. *Infinitives*
    English variant: John asked *to* see it
    Patois variant: John aks *fi* see it
11. *Negatives*
    English variant: The boy doesn't see it
    Patois variant: Di boy no want it

---

4 and 5. The remaining five subjects were in fact very heavy Patois users. It would seem that the reading and initial discussion of the questionnaires, which necessitated at least a measure of English usage, had a more noticeable effect on the index scores of heavy than light Patois users, and that, in the absence of this conversational topic, Patois usage may well have been higher in situation 4 than in situation 5.

Second, the lowest use of Patois is located in situations 1, 2 and 3. In by far the largest number of cases, situation 1, the formal white interview, contains least Patois. It should be noted, however, that for most subjects the

TABLE 5 *Index Scores and Mean Index Scores for all Situations*

Speaker No.	Situation 1	Situation 2	Situation 3	Situation 4	Situation 5
1	100	95.58	98.57	40.27	64.43
2	100	93.65	99.31	77.4	78.49
3	100	97.76	99.33	54.5	93.37
4	100	97.88	98.84	73.44	81.14
5	98.73	97.79	96.85	74.77	91.06
6	100	91.98	98	74.98	80.9
7	96.43	97.71	95.45	75.15	95.03
8	98.36	96.81	96.93	76.69	74.2
9	99.36	96.41	98.14	57.74	92.84
10	97.39	97.77	95.71	62.47	76.66
11	98.82	96.58	98.45	75.67	77.63
12	99.07	90.73	96.16	50.35	57.73
13	99.61	97.55	98.73	42.68	76.08
14	99.58	96.19	97.31	75.76	79.09
15	97.01	96.7	94.17	39.53	68.6
16	83.14	93.72	88.43	63.52	27.32
17	94.95	98.67	96	70.68	80.09
18	96.27	97.29	96.5	52.53	66.05
19	99.18	100	97.72	68.54	89.19
20	98.13	93.91	96.65	86.88	91.73
21	97.31	99.17	99.03	80.14	96.23
22	100	94.12	98.41	*	94.16
23	98.33	57.93	94.11	20.02	47.69
24	84.85	64.69	52.24	3.5	7.87
25	100	97.22	99.69	68	92.9
26	100	100	100	69.74	92.51
27	99.54	100	99.75	77.57	97.26
28	92.71	91.06	96.87	40.27	71.05
29	94.72	90.68	93.62	37.75	75.88
30	*	*	*	40.24	57.34
31	99.09	99.48	100	72.38	70.92
32	64.31	20.15	51.63	36.75	15.22
33	66.35	41.36	92.01	27.19	18.04
34	98.54	94.93	99.03	61.05	80.85
35	97.14	100	100	86.47	95.1
36	100	100	100	91.18	89.67
37	99.53	96.88	99.27	90.53	95.26
38	100	100	99.2	78.88	86.28
39	100	100	100	84.57	90.14
40	97.54	67.14	96.57	28.84	47.44
41	100	95.88	98.79	39.46	83.17
42	100	94.52	94.79	39.46	78.67
43	61.87	48.24	76.18	12.24	3.41
44	71.28	25.32	51.24	9.93	12.73
45	75.74	26.91	34.71	5.66	3.7
Mean:	94.43	87.05	92.37	56.71	69.89

*Empty cells indicate insufficient speech for analysis.

difference between the index scores for these three situations was very small. With the exception of subjects 16, 24, 32, 33, 43, 44 and 45, index scores for all speakers in all three situations ranged between 90 and 100, and most were located near 100. Any reduction from this maximum score can be attributed to the presence of a limited number of features, including the Patois phonological variants, and uninflected nouns (see Chapter 9 for further discussion of this point). Thus, the majority of speakers tended to view the white formal interview as the most "English" situation. Ethnic solidarity with the black interviewer was reflected in the cases of some two thirds of the sample in situation 2 by the choice of a wider range of Patois features, and the same proportion monitored out fewer Patois features in the informal racially mixed conversation than in the formal white interview. It should be stressed, however, that the magnitude of the differences between the index scores for these three situations is seldom large.

Patois frequency scores

Examination of the mean index score for each situation thus gives a very clear indication of the ways in which formality and ethnicity affect language use. However, we were also interested in correlating linguistic behaviour with the various other background variables considered in Chapter 5 and, for a number of reasons, it was more appropriate to attempt these correlations with a single measure rather than with five separate index scores. One problem related to the distribution of the data. The individual Patois indices have a very skewed distribution, with many values near 100 and a few much lower. This creates several problems for statistical analysis. The standard angular transformation (see, for example, Snedecor & Cochran, 1967) was used to stabilize variances, but residuals still revealed a marked non-normality, making it difficult to interpret the exact values of sums of squares. Whereas the relationship between Patois frequency and situation emerges quite clearly from a consideration of the means and the related discussion above, a statistical analysis of the relationship between the Patois indices and other background variables, such as sex and education, is not feasible because of the precise nature of the linguistic data.

A second problem concerned the ordering of the different situations. It was not possible to randomize this order because we wanted to maximize the informality of situations 4, where subjects were alone, and 5, where they were talking informally with the black researcher. It would not have been possible, for instance, to have started recording with either of these situations if we wished to obtain authentically informal speech. An attempt was made to monitor any order effects, however, by switching the formal white interview from the beginning to the end of the recording. Although there were no indications that this change affected the index scores of participants (see Appendix 2 for more detailed statistical discussion), it would not be possible to say with certainty that any effects noted are not order effects unless the different situations had been randomized to different subjects.

A measure of the overall frequency of Patois usage, the *Patois frequency score*, was therefore devised, based on the mean index scores of subjects for all five situations. The background variables considered were education, sex, network and acquiescence–criticalness. As was the case for the index scores discussed above, the lower the score, the higher the frequency of Patois variants in a participant's speech.

Analysis was carried out using analysis of variance (see Appendix 2). Three variables — acquiescence–criticalness (significance level: $>1\%$), the interaction of education and sex (significance level: $>1\%$) and network (significance level: 1%) — had a statistically significant effect on the Patois frequency scores.

Acquiescence–criticalness

A statistically significant correlation was established between language and attitudes towards mainstream white society, in such a way that those young people who viewed white society negatively also tended to be among the heaviest users of Patois features. Although the speakers in the sample were unanimous on some issues, such as their disapproval of the way in which the police treat black people, there was a very wide range of opinions as to how black people should respond to this treatment. Some participants said that they would try and get away if they were stopped and questioned by the police; some thought they would co-operate but complain; others felt the best course of action would be to co-operate without complaint. Attitudes towards other aspects of mainstream white society also varied a good deal. Whereas everyone felt that at least some teachers were racially prejudiced, some young people considered their time in school was happy; others had been suspended for unacceptable behaviour, triggered by what the young people perceived to be a racist treatment.

It is interesting to note that the scale of acquiescence–criticalness suggested by the work of Fuller (1983) has proved to be a powerful analytical tool which by-passes many of the difficulties raised by the more traditional life style approaches discussed in Chapter 2. Thus, while previous formulations which linked the use of Patois with black youth culture (cf. Hebdige, 1976) can be seen to be too broad and simplistic, they nevertheless draw attention to an important social determinant of linguistic behaviour: the more critical the speaker's attitudes towards white

society, the greater the likelihood of a high proportion of Patois features in
their speech.

The interaction of sex and education

The statistically significant effect of the interaction of sex and education
on Patois frequency should be interpreted with caution. Education had
originally been scored on a scale of 0–10, but plots of Patois frequency scores
against education showed that it is in fact better taken as a 2-level factor
(1:<5, 2: >5). It is interesting to note that a score of 5 or more indicates that
subjects have educational qualifications of at least O-level standard.

FIGURE 5 *Plot of Patois Frequency Against Education Scores for Male and
Female Speakers*

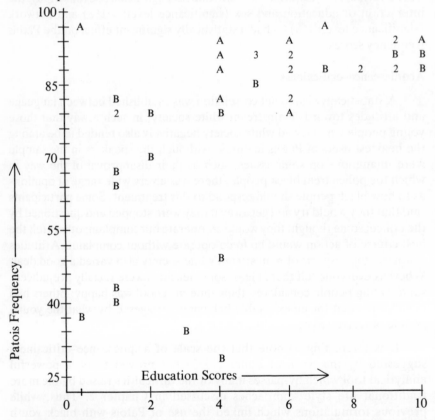

If education or sex alone are considered they can be seen to have an
effect on Patois frequency. The significant interaction between these
factors, however, shows that the size of the education effect is different for

males and females. Examination of the estimates shows that increasing education scores have no effect on the frequency with which female speakers use Patois, but decrease the frequency of Patois in male speakers. However, the low-scoring education group included only five young women. This bias in the sample is not at all surprising in view of educational statistics which point to higher levels of educational achievement for girls than for boys (cf. Driver, 1980). Thus, although the interaction of sex and education has proved to be significant for this particular sample, it cannot necessarily be assumed that the same would be the case if the sample had included a larger number of low-achieving females.

Social network

The network scores achieved by the various young people in the sample are a measure of integration into the black community. Sometimes the degree of integration is a matter of choice; on other occasions it is a function of circumstances. Many black youngsters have no choice about where they live or whether they work and these structural forces clearly constrain their social relations with white people. Within this framework, however, there is a degree of choice. Individuals are free to decide whether to associate with white neighbours or white friends from school. If they are in employment, they can choose whether or not they wish to meet work-mates socially. The various alternatives open to young people, either through choice or circumstances, vary a great deal and are reflected in a wide range of network scores.

Social relations can potentially exert an important normative force over all aspects of behaviour, including language. It seems reasonable to hypothesize, for instance, that young people who form a part of extremely closed social networks, characterized by dense and multiplex bonds within the group, will be subject to considerably greater pressure to conform than those who have a looser network structure. The present analysis confirms this hypothesis: the greater the degree of integration into the black community the more frequent the use of Patois.

The normative power of social network over language could be seen quite clearly on a number of occasions during recording. The most dramatic example came in the white researcher's formal interview with Tommy, Don and Paddy, the three heaviest Patois users in the sample. Although the three young men used a wide range of Patois features throughout the interview, their frequency was much lower than in the other situations. The index scores ranging between 61 and 75 for the three speakers indicated much higher Patois frequency in the white interview situation for these speakers than for any other young people in the sample. However, when the same speakers were chatting informally to the black fieldworkers, English variants almost completely disappeared and index scores dropped between 3 and 13. Thus, while their most formal speech still showed a high frequency of Patois features, they had nonetheless adapted their speech to the formal situation to a significant degree.

The tension which this generated within the group was plain to see. When Tommy is being interviewed, Don interjects:

"You watch how he talk English, how he sound daft. Im sound daft, you know."

When it is Don's turn to answer questions, he prefaces his replies with:

"Hear di difference dough when me talking, hear di difference now. A true blackman dis, you know. True blackman, dis. . . . You should coulda talk as nice as me dough."

In the course of the interview, Don makes the unfortunate mistake of using the English word "hit" instead of Patois "lick". Tommy quickly seizes on this opportunity to retaliate, but Don can only offer a feeble defence:

Don: Unless hard time hit him.
Tommy: Talk Patois, man, you sound daft. "Unless hard time lick
             him".
Don: Di man can't understand we — he can't understand we.

The particular value of the network analysis lies in its explanatory power. It might have been possible, for instance, to do an analysis of the present data purely in terms of the sex of the speaker, and statistically significant differences would undoubtedly have emerged. If this course had been adopted, however, we would have been faced with an *observation* about language behaviour rather than an *explanation* and could only have speculated whether the differences could be attributed to an inherent quality of masculinity or femininity, or some other factor. The present analysis demonstrates that, even when the effect of sex is removed, there is a statistically significant relationship between social network and Patois frequency. It draws attention to the normative influence which close-knit social groups can exert on their members and has the added advantage of showing that any differences between the young men and women in the sample can be explained in terms of different patterns of social network associated with both sexes.

Three case studies

The approach employed in the analysis above is heavily quantitative. Studies of this kind are often able to discern regularities in the data which might not otherwise be apparent. Statistical analysis has the added advantage of being able to demonstrate whether any observed regularities are due to genuine effects or merely chance fluctuations of the data. However, the very act of abstracting patterns can have a fragmentary effect on our understanding of what takes place. In focussing on the overall picture it is sometimes possible to lose sight of the individuals who form the starting point for the study.

Three case studies of very different young people are presented below in an attempt to redress any imbalance produced by the quantitative approach which characterizes the early part of this chapter. Don, Polly and Darleen have a wide range of educational backgrounds, attitudes towards mainstream society and network relations. They also differ considerably in the frequency with which they use Patois variants in their speech. Their cases can thus usefully illustrate in more personal terms the trends and patterns which have emerged in the quantitative analysis above.

Don

Don is 20. He is popular, confident and takes great care in his appearance. His taste in clothes draws admiring comments from his friends. As Don himself remarks, "Mi pop style often, all di time."

His time at school was not particularly happy. He admits that he was lazy and quite difficult to deal with but points to various incidents, all of a racist nature, which demonstrate the unfair treatment which he sometimes received. For instance:

"One time we was at school and the bell went. We all sort of slide out and this white boy drop a packet of empty crisp paper and, before the teacher tell him to pick it up, a me im a ask. And me say: 'Me na pick it up' and im goes: 'Pick it up' and me never pick it up."

Nevertheless his hostility was reserved for only certain teachers and he reckons that less than half of the staff were prejudiced. He left school without taking any exams and has no plans to take any in the future.

When he left school he found a job spot-welding. He worked with the same firm for a year before he was sacked, and talked freely about the reasons for his dismissal. He felt, for instance, that white workers often "skived" and saw no reason why he should not do the same. He started taking half days off and coming into work late. He was warned first and then asked to leave. However, a year later he was offered his old job back and worked there for a further 12 months without incident before the firm went bankrupt and he was made redundant. He had been unemployed for almost a year when recording took place.

Don's attitude towards mainstream white society are among the most hostile in the sample. He dislikes the social isolation of whites in a multi-cultural society:

> "If you go to college, you see Indian, Pakistani, Greek, Blackman, Chinese all mix together. Then you look see the white kids them over there."

He also feels insulted by whites who suggest that blacks should go back to "their own country". He finds the treatment of black people by the police very unfair and says that if he were stopped and questioned he would not hesitate to try and get away. He considers the media coverage of black people to be equally shameful:

> "If it's for a crime it's a blackman. If it's a mugging it's a blackman. Why has it got to be a blackman?"

His family are Pentecostal Christians. He goes to church occasionally, mainly to pacify his parents, but he is not a committed Christian. His contacts with white people have been minimal since leaving work and extend to the occasional conversation with white school friends. He never has any social contact with white neighbours. Most of his time is spent in a very tight knit and exclusively black circle of friends. At weekends they visit black nightclubs and dance to reggae, funk and electric funk. They spend time together at the snooker club and playing sport. They used to be very involved in a black youth club which has now been closed down by the council. They occasionally visit the new black youth club which has replaced it, but feel it doesn't really compare with the old one.

Don's life thus centres very firmly on the black community. This is reflected in a very high network score which correlates with high scores on all the linguistic measures. Don uses Patois in all five situations included in the recording, a pattern found in only five other people in the sample. His use of Patois is predictably highest in conversations where all the participants are black. After completing the questionnaire, for instance, Don offers his candid opinions to the black fieldworker and the other participants:

> "Dem [the questions] alright in a way, right. Dem reasonable. Dem coulda be lickle better, but dem reasonable. Me na bex (angry) wid dem, dem alright. . . . When white people ready fi write some rubbish bout black people, dem can do it, dem can do it, right. So dat's why me say dem reasonable. Notn wrong wid dem."

This short extract illustrates a wide range of the features in the Patois index. The phonology is consistently Patois; he uses Patois pronouns *mi* and *dem*; adjectival verbs *bex*, *reasonable* and *alright*; *fi* before an infinitive; and *no* in negative constructions. Elsewhere in the same conversation he also uses a number of Patois features not included in the index. For instance, when explaining that he has just lost some tickets for a dance he says:

"Me still naa get in, mi still naa get in because a na fi-dem fault. Dat no have notn fi do wid dem."
(I still won't get in, I still won't get in because it's not THEIR fault. That hasn't got anything to do with them.)

He uses the focussing particle *a* and the Patois possessive *fi-dem*. And when explaining some Patois expressions he says:

"Me say, 'Do it! Flash it!' Dat mean seh im a go beat im."
(I say, 'Do it, Flash it!' That means he's going to beat him.)

Here he uses the continuative particle *a*, and *seh* which in Patois follows psychic state transitive verbs. His most "English" performance, in contrast, is in the formal white interview. When talking about the origins of black culture, for instance, he says:

"I say it come from Africa really. It started from dere tru slavery. Dat's di way I see it. It started from there, yeah. But those kids what born over here right, they don't want to admit it. Like Paddy, they don't want to admit it right that our culture started from Africa."

Don's language in this situation is highly variable. Whereas in black peer group conversation he shows an overwhelming preference for Patois variants, in the white interview he chooses a much higher proportion of English variants including inflected past tenses, negatives with *don't* and copulas. While he still uses Patois features like dental stops (*tru, dere, di*) and adjectival verbs (*born*), the number and range of these features is very limited.

Polly

Polly is 18. She left school before taking any public exams, but is actively considering taking evening classes to get some recognized qualifications. She is currently unemployed, but has done two Youth Opportunity Project placements in catering, each lasting six months. She is keen to find work as soon as possible: "The days are too boring."

Polly is a good deal less hostile towards mainstream white society than Don. For instance, she opposes the idea of separate clubs for blacks and

whites on the grounds that this is unnecessary segregation. Nonetheless, she
is very critical of the police handling of black people and various aspects of
education. She points out that when she was at school she never learned
anything about black language or culture. She feels that Black Studies
should be made widely available and taught to both black and white pupils.
She also draws attention to the question of black children and sport and the
unfortunate implications for achievement in academic subjects of high
teacher expectations of black pupils in this area:

> "Our netball team was mainly black girls. Instead of going to, say,
> the French lesson, we'd go and practise."

Her social networks are mainly black. She sees white friends occasionally but never visits white neighbours. She has a close circle of black friends
and their main interest, like Don and his friends, is visiting black night clubs.
Although many of her friends are Christians, she is not a regular Church-
goer.

The very different social profile which emerges for Polly is faithfully
reflected in very different language behaviour. Don distinguishes between
"English" and "Patois" situations by decreasing the relative proportions of
Patois variants in the more "English" situations, but nonetheless retains a
high proportion of Patois variants irrespective of the situation. Polly, however, monitors out all Patois variants from situations in which white speakers
are present. Her phonology is unmistakeably West Midlands and she also
shows evidence of non-standard British English grammar. When defending
Rastafarianism, for instance, she says:

> "Oh no, it depends. You've got to get to know them . . . I mean
> like, say, with my Mum, right. She just saw some and said, 'Oh,
> he's no good', cos he'd got locks on his head. You know Junior
> Palmer? I tell you, him and my Mum! When my Mum got to know
> him, the two of them, they were like that. Junior couldn't do
> nothing wrong. You know love, Junior was gold.

In contrast, Polly's Patois in black speech situations is impressive. She
uses a very wide range of Patois features and her delivery is fast and fluent.
However, whereas Don sustains the use of Patois in black situations, Polly
switches frequently between "English" and "Patois" (italicized in the example below). This switching may take place even within the same sentence
and it often achieves dramatic or amusing effects:

> "With Melanie right, you have to say she speaks *tri different sort of*
> *language when she want to. Cos she speak half Patois, half English*
> *and when im ready im will come out wid,* 'I day and I bay and I ay

this and I ay that. I day have it and I day know where it is' . . . And then she goes, '*Lord God, I so hot*'. Now she'll be sitting there right and she'll go, 'It's hot, isn't it?', you know, and you think which one is he going to grow up speaking?"

Darleen

Darleen is 18. She left school with some CSEs and hopes to do some O-levels in evening classes. She is currently unemployed but has recently finished a six month Youth Opportunities Project as an auxiliary nurse. She very much enjoyed the work and would now like to train as a state registered nurse.

Her time at school was generally very enjoyable. She lives on a council estate where there are very few black families and went to the neighbourhood school. Her attitude towards British Black people suggests that she has internalized many of the prejudices which are prevalent in mainstream white society:

"Black people, they don't try to better themselves, they'm still going on the same culture what's been going on for ages. They never come out of it . . . Ganja, girls and nothing else, and stealing."

Darleen's social networks include both blacks and whites. Many of her close school friends were white, and she also has a certain amount of social contact with white neighbours. As she herself comments, "We'm brought up in a white community." However, two out of her three best friends are black and she does attend a black youth club.

Darleen's knowledge of several aspects of black language and culture is limited. She was unfamiliar with dub, a very important black musical innovation, knew no Patois proverbs and had to ask for an explanation of "popping style" when she was completing the questionnaire. She used Patois variants with considerably less frequency than either Don or Polly. None of the situations except the black peer conversation, when she was left alone with her friends, showed any evidence of Patois variants at all. Her English was marked not only by the non-standard British features which were found in Polly's speech but by a high incidence of specifically Black Country dialect forms such as *her, wor, cor, ay* and copulas in *(a)m*. In describing facilities for young people in Dudley, for instance, she says:

"Just walk up the streets and you'm out of Dudley, know what I mean? In Birmingham, I don't know, I just get round a nice shop — I'm lost in it. But if you just walk up the High Street you'm out . . .

> The other best thing in Dudley is the Trident Centre, that's what I think, there by Sainsbury's. You can sit down there. I said to Michael today, 'That's the best thing in Dudley, ay it?' "

The only time when Darleen uses Patois is when left alone with her friends. Close examination of her speech with friends shows that her code-switching behaviour is not nearly as well developed as that of Polly and most of her speech is unambiguously "English". She shows only a narrow range of Patois features, making variable use of Patois dentals and vowels and uninflected nouns and verbs. Otherwise Patois is limited to *mi, im, dem* and the continuative particle *a*:

> "Wa happen? Me a go say you a go get what you a look for?"
> *(What happened? I'm going to say that you're going to get what you're looking for.)*

She is very aware of the limitations in her Patois:

> "Tell the truth, we'm very up on our English. We talk slang sometime in Patois. . . . If I was in Jamaica now I'd be brought up to talk like that, but it's a white community."

These case studies show both the strengths and limitations of an analysis in terms of the frequency of occurrence of Patois variants. The relationship between attitudes towards mainstream white society, and network relations and educational aspirations and achievement on the one hand, and Patois frequency on the other, emerge very clearly, and the young people's own comments help to give substance to the general trends and patterns abstracted in the quantitative analysis earlier in the chapter. Various aspects of their language behaviour, however, cannot be captured by correlations with Patois frequency. It is evident, for instance, that different speakers command a different range of Patois features, and it is important to explore any social or linguistic constraints on the range of competence which exists within the British Black community. This is a theme which will be pursued in Chapter 8. It is also evident that Patois variants are distributed quite differently not only from speaker to speaker but from situation to situation. The symbolic significance of the patterns which emerge will be considered in Chapter 9.

Summary

Measures of the relative frequencies of Patois and English variants can thus be used in a number of ways. They indicate the effects of formality and ethnicity over the whole sample; they also point to differences in response to situational variation between speakers. It was clear, for instance, that the two informal black situations — when speakers were left alone (situation 4) and when they chatted to the black researcher (situation 5) — contained a significantly higher proportion of Patois variants than the formal interviews (situations 1 and 2) or the informal racially mixed conversation (situation 3). There were also subtle differences between individual speakers' treatment of the situations which emerged as more "English". Although there was a high degree of agreement that the formal interview was the most English situation, the picture concerning situations 2 and 3 was more confused. Some speakers used a slightly higher proportion of Patois variants to indicate ethnic solidarity with the black interviewer; some people marked the informality of the racially mixed conversation in the same way. There are certainly indications of different patterns emerging for different speakers and this is a theme which is developed further in Chapter 9.

Because of the difficulties of studying the relationships between individual Patois index scores and background variables, an overall measurement of the relative proportions of English and Patois, the *frequency score*, was devised. Attitudes towards mainstream white society were found to have a statistically significant effect on Patois frequency, the most critical speakers tending to have the highest frequency of Patois features. In the present sample, the interaction between sex and education was also found to have a statistically significant effect on Patois frequency. Thus, while education did not appear to affect the scores of the young women, high achieving young men showed fewer Patois features in their speech than did the male low achievers. This may be an artefact, in part at least, of a sample which contained a very small number of low-achieving females. There can be little doubt, however, as to the strong effect of social networks on language behaviour: if individuals have strong network ties with other black people, their speech is likely to contain a high proportion of Patois features.

Three case studies, based on young people with very different social characteristics and patterns of languge behaviour are used to give substance to the patterns which have emerged in the quantitative sociolinguistic analysis. They are also used to indicate the weaknesses of an analysis purely in terms of Patois frequency. Such an analysis tells us nothing, for instance, of the range of competence in Patois which exists within the British Black community, nor of the different patterns of language choice and their symbolic significance. These are themes which will be pursued in the following chapters.

8 The notion of "competence" and the Patois speaker

So far we have tried to characterize the language behaviour of British Black people in terms of the frequency with which they use particular Patois variants. However, the picture which has emerged is necessarily partial. It reveals no information, for instance, on the nature of differences in Patois competence which may exist from speaker to speaker. It might also lead us to suppose that the young people who used Patois variants most frequently were those whose understanding of the grammar of Patois was most complete. Close examination of the range of Patois variants used by different speakers shows this to be an overly simplistic interpretation of the facts of Patois usage. In this chapter we will be considering the various degrees of Patois competence which are to be found among British Black speakers, the social characteristics of those speakers and the implications of these findings for an understanding of the language behaviour of a speech community.

"Competence" and "performance"

Before proceeding to these questions, an explanatory note needs to be appended on the particular use of competence in the present discussion. The distinction between "competence" and "performance" was originally proposed by Chomsky (1965). He argued that "competence" should be reserved for speakers' knowledge of their language, and "performance" for their use of the language in a given situation. This distinction has given rise to a great deal of confusion and criticism (see Katz, 1981; Fillmore *et al.*, 1979; Matthews, 1979, Bresnan & Kaplan, 1982; Milroy, 1984, for a sample of the kind of objections which have been raised). The competence–performance distinction comes under particularly ferocious attack from linguists who are working with the "diffuse" linguistic data which is characteristic of multi-

94

lingual situations, or situations in which non-standard varieties co-exist with the standard. Writers like Klein & Dittmar (1979), for instance, object on the grounds that the distinction has no relevance for a wide range of theoretically interesting situations, such as pidgins and child language.

In a discussion of British Black speakers, we are concerned with differences which exist between individuals in the ability to speak Patois. The word which springs to mind most readily in this context is "competence", in the non-technical rather than the Chomskyan sense. In this respect, my position is the same as that of Hymes (1979: 41):

> " 'Competence' is the most normal and natural word for the abilities of individuals. The difficulty with Chomsky's use was that the term was, in effect, redefined so as to apply only to a part of the abilities of a person, and so as to imply an equation between the object of theory that bore the name 'English' and individual abilities. . . . We know, of course, that the abilities of individuals are both more and less than was implied by Chomsky's notion: more in that they comprise more than grammar, often more than a single variety or indeed language; less, in that it is in the nature of the social division of labor and the contingency of experience that the systematic potential of the language as a whole exceeds the command of any one person. It seems to me desirable to reinstitute the term 'competence' in the study of individual differences."

For the purposes of the present discussion, therefore, "competence" will be used to refer to language abilities in general.

The Patois competence score

Any assessment of Patois competence must be a function of how large a portion of the phonology and grammar individual speakers command rather than how frequently they use Patois variants. This poses certain difficulties. First, the assessment needs to address itself to both phonology and syntax, and, as the discussion in Chapter 4 made clear, syntactic variants occur with far less frequency than phonological variants. In the construction of the Patois index, for instance, it was necessary to restrict discussion to those variants which occurred relatively frequently throughout the sample. However, since we are now interested in *whether* and not *how often* a speaker produces a particular variant, the inclusion of relatively infrequently occurring syntactic variables clearly gives rise to far fewer problems. Secondly, some young people spoke less than others and so there was the possibility that the smaller quantities of speech would be an imperfect reflection of the speakers' actual competence. It was possible, however, to determine statistically the effect of the amount of speech uttered on Patois competence.

A Patois competence score was thus devised. It was based on some 20 features of Patois phonology and grammar. Of these, certain features included in the Patois Index have already been discussed in Chapter 6. Close examination of the transcripts enabled us to identify a range of additional Patois variants including questions, focus, and psychic state transitive verbs, which marked the speech of a relatively small proportion of speakers. It was evident that the occurrence of these additional features offered interesting possibilities both for distinguishing between speakers and for understanding any implicational relations which might hold between different variants. Speakers scored one point for each of the 20 Patois features which occurred in their speech, irrespective of how often these features appeared.

Patois competence scale

Examination of the data revealed a great deal of variation between speakers with scores ranging from 8 to 20. This is a phenomenon which has attracted limited attention in the literature. Thomas (1979), for instance,

FIGURE 6　*Distribution of Competence Scores*

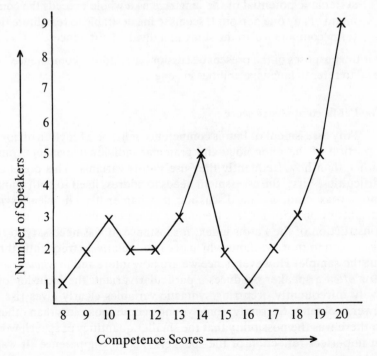

comments that children's use of Patois ranges from a few stock phrases copied from their mothers' rebukes or pop songs to the ability to hold long conversations. Sebba (1984c) also notes the varying degrees of fluency to be found among young London black people. Previous discussions, however, have tended to be impressionistic.

TABLE 6 *Patois Features in the Competence Scale*

1. *Dentals*
   /t, d/, e.g. /tik, dat/ — thick, that
2. *Vowels*
   /o/, e.g. /fon/ — fun
3. *Third person singular present tense verbs*
   John *swim* fast, Kevin *eat* a lot
4. *Plurals*
   six *car*
5. *Simple past tense*
   Winston *see* di boy; Beverley *walk* away
6. *First person singular pronoun*
   mi feel happy
7. *Third person singular pronouns*
   im put im coat away
8. *Third person plural pronouns*
   dem see di baby; look at *dem* hat
9. *Negatives*
   Di boy no see it — the boy doesn't see it
10. *Adjectival verbs*
    Di man *happy* — the man is happy
11. *Continuatives*
    John *a come* — John is coming
12. *Focus*
    A John do it — *John* did it/it was John who did it
13. *Questions*
    Mary a go home? — Is Mary going home?
    Harvey see di man? — Did Harvey see the man?
14. *Infinitives*
    John aks *fi* see it — John asked to see it
15. *Other pronouns*
    Unu want it — you (plural) want it
    Give me *fi-dem* book — give me their books
16. *Psychic state transitive verbs*
    Tony tell me *seh* im no know — Tony told me he didn't know
17. *'-dem' plurals*
    Give me *di* book-*dem*
18. *Locating verb*
    Mary *deh* a yaad — Mary is at home
19. *Equating verb*
    Patrick *a* di winner — Patrick is the winner
20. *Past markers*
    Roy *did* ready in di morning — Roy was getting ready in the morning

Speakers' own comments reflected a keen awareness of the extent of their own — and other people's — competence. At the one extreme, Rory responded to a question about the language of the home with:

"Every minute, every minute, a just pure Patois mi speak when mi inna yard."

Teddy explained that he sometimes felt uncomfortable speaking English:

"When I'm at home I speak Patois, but when I'm at work I automatically go back to English . . . but if it get too much for me, me just cut down to Patois."

At the other extreme, Darleen admits to the limitations in her ability to speak Patois. She also talks of her embarrassment at not always understanding other people:

"Sometimes when I speak to a Rasta guy I cannot speak Patois because I feel I'm going to slip up and feel stupid. If a chap says to me, 'You a go burn fire, mi a go deal you a dis, dat' I think, 'I ay heard that saying before.' I feel div[1] and I'm thinking, 'What's he saying?'"

Comments such as these are in fact supported by objective measures of the speakers' competence. It is important, however, to interpret these comments with a fair degree of caution. Earlier in the same conversation, Darleen and her friend Beccy give a very different impression of her abilities:

Beccy: When she talks Patois you can hardly understand her.
Darleen: I talk so fast, I do talk fast when I'm talking Patois.
Beccy: It's like when you went to get them questionnaires, her got carried away. . . .

Similarly, Julie who is objectively a competent Patois speaker, chose to underplay her abilities:

"When my friend-dem say — my coloured friends that used to talk to me — 'Wa happen to you, you can't speak Patois?' I said, 'Yeah, I know.' Especially the black boys down our road when they say, 'You alright, sis?' Me say, 'Oh, I'm fine' . . . 'Wa happen to you? You can't talk Patois? Wa happen? You tink you a white?'"

It would appear that overt comments are not always accurate reflections of the ability to speak Patios.

Table 7 below shows both inter-individual differences and the actual relations which hold between the various Patois features. Along the horizontal axis features are arranged from those used by the highest number of speakers to those used by the lowest. Along the vertical axis, speakers are ordered from those with the highest scores to those with the lowest.

TABLE 7 *Patois Competence Scale*

Speaker Nos.	Dentals	/o/	3rd person present -s	Plurals	Simple past	mi	im	dem	DO+neg	Adjectival verbs	Focus	Questions	Infinitives	Continuatives	Other pronouns	Locating verb	'-dem' plurals	Psychic state verbs	Equating verb	Past marker
43	x	x	x	x	x	x	x	x	x	x	x	x	x	x	x	x	x	x	x	x
44	x	x	x	x	x	x	x	x	x	x	x	x	x	x	x	x	x	x	x	x
40	x	x	x	x	x	x	x	x	x	x	x	x	x	x	x	x	x	x	x	x
34	x	x	x	x	x	x	x	x	x	x	x	x	x	x	x	x	x	x		x
11	x	x	x	x	x	x	x	x	x	x	x	x	x	x	x	x	x	x		x
15	x	x	x	x	x	x	x	x	x	x	x		x	x	x	x	x	x	x	x
41	x	x	x	x	x	x	x	x	x	x	x	x	x	x	x	x	x	x	x	x
33	x	x	x	x	x	x	x	x	x	x	x	x	x	x	x	x	x	x	x	x
16	x	x	x	x	x	x	x	x	x	x	x	x	x	x	x	x	x	x	x	x
23	x	x	x	x	x	x	x	x	x	x	x	x	x	x	x	x	x	x	x	x
29	x	x	x	x	x	x	x	x	x	x	x	x	x	x	x	x	x	x	x	x
18	x	x	x	x	x	x	x	x	x	x	x	x	x	x	x	x	x	x	x	x
4	x	x	x	x	x	x	x	x	x		x	x	x	x	x	x	x	x	x	x
12	x	x	x	x	x	x	x	x	x	x	x		x	x	x	x	x	x	x	x
24	x	x	x	x	x	x	x	x	x	x	x	x			x	x	x	x	x	x
31	x	x	x	x	x	x	x	x	x	x	x	x	x	x	x	x		x	x	
7	x	x	x	x	x	x	x	x	x	x	x	x	x	x	x	x		x	x	
13	x	x	x	x	x	x	x	x	x	x	x	x	x	x	x	x		x	x	
32	x	x	x	x	x	x	x	x	x	x	x	x	x	x	x	x	x	x	x	
45	x	x	x	x	x	x	x	x	x	x	x	x	x	x	x	x	x	x		
28	x	x	x	x	x	x	x	x	x	x	x	x	x	x	x	x		x		
6	x	x	x	x	x	x	x		x	x			x	x	x	x	x	x		
10	x	x	x	x	x	x	x	x	x	x	x					x	x	x		
14	x	x	x	x	x	x	x	x	x	x	x	x		x	x			x		
42	x	x	x	x	x	x	x	x	x	x	x	x	x	x	x	x		x		
19	x	x	x	x	x	x		x	x	x	x	x	x	x	x	x				
1	x	x	x	x	x	x	x	x	x	x	x		x	x	x			x		
9	x	x	x	x	x	x	x	x	x	x	x	x		x	x			x		
3	x	x	x	x	x	x	x	x	x	x	x	x	x		x	x				
2	x	x	x	x	x	x	x	x		x	x			x		x			x	x
8	x	x	x	x	x	x	x	x	x	x	x	x		x	x					
26	x	x	x	x	x	x	x	x	x	x			x	x	x					
17	x	x	x	x	x	x	x	x	x		x			x	x					
26	x	x	x	x	x	x	x	x	x		x		x			x				
38	x	x	x	x	x	x	x	x	x		x	x	x	x						
30	x	x	x	x	x	x	x	x	x	x	x	x	x							
35	x	x	x	x	x	x	x		x	x		x	x				x		x	
20	x	x	x	x	x	x	x		x							x	x		x	
21	x	x	x	x	x	x	x	x	x		x			x						
27	x	x	x	x	x	x	x	x	x	x	x									
36	x	x	x	x	x	x	x	x	x		x					x				
39	x	x	x	x	x	x	x	x	x	x										
37	x	x	x	x	x	x							x		x					

Patois as a second language?

For a number of years, there have been teacher reports that some children who show no sign of Patois features in their speech during their early years at school, start using noticeably black speech during adolescence. If this observation is true, it raises a number of important questions. For instance, do we assume that these children have a working knowledge of Patois from infancy but simply choose not to use it in the school situation until much later? Or do they actually acquire Patois much later through contact with other speakers? The present data would suggest that different children follow different routes.

The data displayed in Table 7 show that a little over a third of the sample are very fluent speakers who confidently use the rull range of Patois features. There are obvious differences between the speech of these participants and Patois speakers in Jamaica. British Blacks will show a good deal more code-switching behaviour than Jamaicans and their "black" speech will tend to show less mesolectal variation (see Chapter 4). However, this group of fluent speakers has a very clear notion of what constitutes basilectal Patois and uses a very wide range of the features associated with it in their own speech.

At the other end of the scale, approximately a quarter of the sample can only be described as having limited competence in Patois. It would appear that these speakers have much in common with the semi- or passive bilingual categories proposed by Dorian (1981; 1982). Dorian defines semi-speakers as individuals who have failed to develop full fluency and normal adult proficiency. They are able to construct intelligible sentences and differ in this respect from near passive bilinguals who tend to have a reasonably large vocabulary, but restrict their output to short phrases and single word utterances. There are, however, important differences between the East Sutherland communities described by Dorian and British Black communities. For instance, Dorian describes the frequently ungrammatical utterances produced by semi-speakers. The range of variation between two related systems and the code-switching behaviour which is the norm for even the most competent of speakers makes it possible for speakers to mark a situation as "Patois" using either a narrow or a wide range of features (see Chapter 9). Individuals would therefore seem to be characterized as "good" or as "not so good" speakers on the basis of the range of features which they use rather than on whether or not they make mistakes.

Between these two poles lies a wide range of competence. It is interesting to note, however, that the Patois features are not distributed randomly among the speakers. Although it is not possible to show a neat sequence in which the presence of one feature follows on the next, there would appear to be evidence for the banding of different groups of features. This banding would allow us to make statements about the implicational relationships between features. It would be possible to say, for instance, that the presence of features belonging to one group confidently predicts the presence of features from the groups below it, but that the reverse relationship is not necessarily so.

The behaviour of these speakers is highly reminiscent of that of second language learners. Acquisition order research for English has shown repeatedly that both adults and children learn structures in a very similar order, and that language learning proceeds by the acquisition of *groups* of structures (Dulay, Burt & Krashen, 1982). Certain individuals show a degree of idiosyncratic variation, and some structures are susceptible to greater variability than others. Nonetheless, there would appear to be a characteristic order for the acquisition of English by second language learners.

An important development in acquisition order research was the application of the Ordering–Theoretic Method (Bart & Krus, 1973) to second language learning (Dulay, Burt & Krashen, 1982). This method makes it possible to identify groups of structures which are acquired at approximately the same time, and to order these groups in relation to one another. Each structure is given a value of 1 if the speaker has acquired it and 0 if it has not been acquired. All structures are then ordered in relation to each other, giving four possible response patterns:

1,1 Both structures have been acquired.
1,0 The first named structure has been acquired, the second has not.
0,1 The first named structure has not been acquired; the second structure has been acquired.
0,0 Neither structure has been acquired.

The hierarchy is determined by establishing which pairs of structures consistently show the 1,0 pattern across subjects. The proportion of "disconfirming cases" (with a 0,1 pattern) is calculated for a given pair of structures, and one construction is said to precede another if 5% or fewer disconfirming cases are found. There are two situations in which structures are considered to form an unordered pair. The first is when they show only a small percentage (usually taken to be 7% or less) of disconfirming cases in *both* directions. The second is when there are 7% or less disconfirming cases in one direction and the proportion of disconfirming cases in the opposite direction is not twice as large.

TABLE 8 *Stair Matrix for the Patois Data*

	Past marker	Equating verb	Locating verb	'-dem' plurals	Psychic state verbs	Other pronouns	Infinitives	Questions	Focus	Continuatives	Adjectival verbs	do+neg	dem	im	mi	Simple past	Plurals	3rd person present -s	/o/	dental
Dentals	+	+	+	+	+	+	+	+	+	+	+	+	+	+						
/o/	+	+	+	+	+	+	+	+	+	+	+	+	+	+						
3rd person present -s	+	+	+	+	+	+	+	+	+	+	+	+	+	+						
Plurals	+	+	+	+	+	+	+	+	+	+	+	+	+	+						
Simple past	+	+	+	+	+	+	+	+	+	+	+	+	+	+						
mi	+	+	+	+	+	+	+	+	+	+	+	+	+	+						
im	+	+	+	+	+	+	+	+	+											
dem	+	+	+	+	+	+	+	+	+											
do+neg	+	+	+	+	+	+	+	+	+											
Adjectival verbs	+	+	+	+	+	+	+	+	+											
Continuatives	+	+	+	+	+	+	+	+	+											
Focus	+	+	+	+	+															
Questions	+	+			(7)															
Infinitives	+	+																		
Other pronouns	+	+																		
Psychic state verbs	+	+																		
'-dem' plurals	+	(7)																		
Locating verb	+	(7)																		
Equating verb																				
Past marker																				

+ denotes 5% or fewer disconfirming cases.   (7) denotes 7% disconfirming cases.

When this method is applied to the Patois data, some very interesting patterns emerge. It is clear that the various features of Patois are learned neither at random nor in isolation. Rather, groups of structures appear to be acquired in set orders across a population of speakers. Table 8 shows a stair matrix which displays the various acquisitional hierarchies. These hierarchies can be best displayed as a simple succession of structures.

The current situation in Britain for young black speakers is both new and dynamic. We are dealing with a generation which incudes many young people who are fully competent speakers of both a highly focussed variety of

FIGURE 7 *Acquisitional Hierarchies for British Black Speakers*

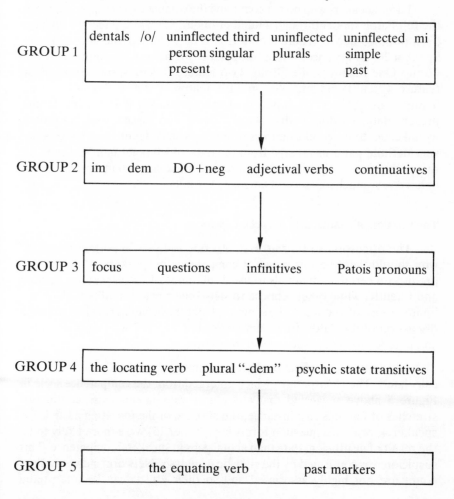

English, indistinguishable or almost indistinguishable from the local white norm, and a variety of Patois very similar to that spoken in Jamaica. The ways in which speakers use this competence, interspersing Patois and English as a part of code-switching behaviour, is very different from anything which we would find in the Caribbean. So, too, is the preference for basilectal rather than mesolectal forms. However, an examination of the actual Patois features concerned shows that many British Black speakers command a range of features very similar to Jamaican speakers. In the absence of longitudinal studies it is impossible to know whether these speakers have always been competent Patois speakers or whether they are highly successful language learners.

Those speakers who do not command the complete range approximate to the full Patois model through a number of quite separate stages which have been outlined above. There are inevitably cases of idiosyncratic variation. Speaker 20, for instance, whose competence in Patois is very limited, uses all Group One features, one Group Two feature ("dem"), one Group Four feature ("seh") and one Group Five feature ("did"). Similarly, some features are subject to a good deal more variation than others. In the present data, locating verbs, plural "-dem" and psychic state transitives would seem to be good examples of more variable features. All the same, very definite patterns emerge from the data which point unmistakeably to the presence of acquisitional hierarchies. Less competent speakers thus behave very much like second language learners.

The relation of competence to social factors

The discussion so far raises an obvious and very important question: why should there be this range of competence in speakers? What factors predispose certain individuals to use a full range of Patois features flexibly and fluently, while others choose to signal their black identity with only a limited range of features? The same explanatory variables considered in the discussion of the Patois frequency scores in Chapter 7 were applied to the competence scores for speakers in the sample.

In addition, the effect of the total length of speakers' utterances was calculated. The clear pattern which emerged from the competence scale in Figure 5 above suggested that any empty cells in otherwise continuous stretches of features (for instance, the absence of the focussing particle for speaker 4, or Patois question forms for speaker 15) were more likely to be the result of insufficient data than actual gaps in speakers' competence. This suspicion was confirmed by the statistical analysis. Network and vocabulary count are not highly associated and so their effects can be interpreted separately. The effect of the vocabulary count on competence scores was found to be significant at the 1% level. This source of variation was removed and network relations emerged as by far the most important effect on Patois competence (significance level: <0.1%).

The degree of speakers' integration into the black community as measured by their network score would thus appear to be the most important determinant of their Patois competence. The opportunity to be with other Patois speakers and to both hear and use Patois is obviously critical. It should be remembered, however, that although all black people have many opportunities for *hearing* Patois around them in the home, from other young black people and in the lyrics of reggae and dub, their opportunities for *using* Patois may be more limited.

Some outside observers have sometimes assumed that there is a simple dichotomy whereby black children use Patois at home and English at school. Writers like Sutcliffe (1982a), however, have shown that, although parents and older people may speak Patois to children, there is a strong expectation within the home that children should speak English to their elders. This position is certainly supported by the young people in the present study. Daryl explains the situation thus:

"When the parents come over from Jamaica, them speak Patois, and the white men they never understand them. So they think that fi-dem kids born here should be able to be more part of society and be able to be understood by the people more than them, so that we would be able to get more ahead in life than them."

But despite this appreciation of the parental position, many British born black people feel that they must agree to differ. Some parents would appear to have far too simplistic a view of the social forces to which their children are exposed and underestimate the importance of Patois in their children's lives. Comments made by the young people in our sample suggest that their exhortations frequently fall on deaf ears.

"Dem a stop me and say, 'We bring you over here fi h'educate you, a learn fi speak better', and all this kind of thing. Well, me used to listen to dem, but after dem gone, me used to speak the same."

There would also appear to be almost universal amusement at their attempts to enforce English usage on their children:

"Every couple of months mum will go, 'Look at Mrs Grant or somebody's children down the road, they speak lovely Henglish. A what wrong with unu?' . . . Then we go, 'How now brown cow, the rain in Spain stays mainly on the plain.' So she goes, 'A what you a do? Lef me alone!'"

Thus while all young black people are likely to hear Patois from their elders in the home, there is a very strong expectation that they should use English and not Patois. Whilst it is reasonable to assume that all or almost all British Black people have a receptive competence (cf. Troike, 1969) in Patois because of this exposure in the home, it would appear that it is the nature of their peer networks which determines to a large extent the opportunities for developing their productive competence.

Life chances open to young black people predispose them to spending more of their time in the company of other black people than in the company of whites. Patterns of settlement imposed by the availability of work and the level of income (see Chapter 2) mean that most black people live in areas where there is a high ethnic minority population. Friendships based on a given locality are necessarily strengthened when schools are organized on a neighbourhood basis. When the level of unemployment is particularly high among young black people they will inevitably spend their time in the company of other unemployed friends, most of whom will be black. It is largely academic to speculate on the degree to which such friendships are based on choice or result from structural factors such as those just outlined.

There is nonetheless considerable inter-individual variation in the relative strengths of black and white social networks. Some young people lived on a predominantly white council estate; some were high academic achievers and chose to pursue further and higher education; some worked in places where they were the only blacks. The exposure of these speakers to Patois, and their opportunities for using it are necessarily far more limited than those of speakers who spend almost all their time in the company of other black people.

Community views on Patois usage

Two questions were put to participants about Patois usage when they were left alone with the questionnaire towards the end of recording. The first related to estimates of their own Patois usage; the second to community usage. In response to the first question:

Do *you* talk Patois often/sometimes/never?

young people were divided between "often" (61%; n=27) and "sometimes" (19%; n=17). Not a single person claimed that they never spoke Patois. Estimates of community usage were also high. Some 57% of the participants (n=25) thought that all or almost all of the British Black population could speak Patois; 23% (n=10) estimated that this proportion was more than half; and only 20% (n=9) thought that half or less could speak Patois. All the young people thus claim to speak Patois often or sometimes and most feel that the ability to speak Patois is extremely widespread.

These findings are closer to those reported by Hadi (1976), Sutcliffe (1978; 1982a), Palmer (1981) and Tomlin (1981), who report high levels of Patois usage, than those of Rosen & Burgess (1980), who consider that Patois usage is considerably less prevalent. It has already been suggested (see Chapter 3) that different estimates reflect different methodologies and research designs. The wide range in both frequency of Patois usage and in Patois competence suggests another possible explanation for the highly divergent findings which have been reported. It seems possible that researchers have quite simply been asking the wrong questions. Different speakers achieve different levels of competence in Patois. It is therefore unrealistic to ask whether someone speaks Patois, because "speaking Patois" means different things for different people.

Summary

An attempt has been made to broaden the description of British Black language from a simple discussion of the frequency of Patois usage and its social correlates to the different levels of competence in Patois which exist within the community. There is clearly a relationship between the two measures, inasmuch as the speakers who use a high proportion of Patois variants are likely to be the most competent speakers. The reverse relationship does not, however, necessarily hold true.

A competence score based on the occurrence of some 20 Patois features was calculated for all the young people. About a third of the sample emerge as highly competent Patois speakers; the rest show widely differing degrees of competence and about a quarter can only be described as having very little competence in Patois. A matrix constructed by arranging speakers from most to least competent along one axis, and features from most to least frequent along the other axis, showed clearly that Patois features were not distributed at random across the speakers. Rather they showed evidence of a number of acquisitional hierarchies of the kind discussed in second language acquisitional order research.

Network was found to exert a statistically significant effect on competence, more competent speakers tending to have more solidly black social relations. Although all speakers are very likely to have a passive competence in Patois through listening to parents and other first generation speakers, there is a strong expectation that young people should use English and not Patois with their elders. Their productive abilities would seem to be constrained by their opportunities to use Patois in situations outside the home.

Notes to Chapter 9

1. Used by younger speakers, black and white, to mean "stupid".

9 Patterns of language use

A picture has emerged from previous chapters of a number of social factors which have a strong effect on the language behaviour of young British Blacks. The young people who use Patois features most frequently are those who have the strongest links with other black speakers, who are most critical of mainstream white society and who, in the case of male speakers, tend to underachieve in school. The young people who have greatest competence in Patois are those who have the strongest black social networks. However, this is inevitably a partial picture, and many questions remain unanswered. We have already noted in Chapter 7, for instance, that different speakers appear to follow different patterns of linguistic behaviour. But how can these patterns best be described? It is possible to define a given situation as "Patois" or "English"? And is there any relationship between the patterns which may exist and the various explanatory variables we may wish to consider?

What constitutes Patois usage?

All of the speakers used Patois variants in at least some situations. Although it was usually a simple matter to identify specific examples of Patois phonology, morphology or syntax, it was a good deal more problematic to decide whether an entire situation should be classed as "Patois" or "English". Some speakers showed no evidence at all of the influence of Patois in a given situation. Others sometimes substituted dental stops for fricatives, or used uninflected nouns, but with such infrequency that "English" seemed a far more appropriate label for the situation than "Patois".

Close examination of the data, however, showed a very interesting patterning which provided objective criteria for the classification of a situation as either "English" or "Patois". Table 9 shows the proportion of

109

speakers using the Patois variants of the 11 features which make up the Patois index described in Chapter 7 for each of the five situations in the recordings. These features fall into two distinct blocks. Block One features occur in a high proportion of speakers for situations 1–3 (the formal white interview, the formal black interview and the informal racially mixed conversation), and in almost all speakers for situations 4 and 5 (the two informal black conversations). Block Two features appear in the speech of a low number of speakers in situations 1–3, and a high number of speakers in situations 4 and 5.

TABLE 9 *Proportions of Speakers who Use Patois Variants, Situation by Situation*

	1	2	3	4	5
Block One:					
Dentals	40.99	57.77	62.22	100	97.77
/o/	52.27	57.77	55.55	97.77	97.77
3rd person singular verbs	61.11	63.15	45.16	83.72	90.47
Plurals	52.68	70.45	57.77	86.67	88.88
Block Two:					
Past	25.81	31.43	42.5	77.27	86.66
Copulas/adjectives and verbs	18.75	18.42	18.60	77.78	77.78
1st person singular pronouns	15.55	24.44	17.77	95.55	80.00
3rd person singular pronouns	18.52	21.85	17.07	57.77	65.91
3rd person plural pronouns	12.20	16.28	17.77	42.22	57.17
Infinitives	23.68	19.05	25.58	44.44	59.09
Negatives with DO	14.28	15.38	11.62	64.44	63.64

Various writers (e.g. Labov, 1966; Gal, 1979; Chambers & Trudgill, 1980) have drawn attention to the different patterns of behaviour associated with different linguistic variables. It is possible, for instance, to detect sharp stratification, in which there are marked differences not only between social groups, but within the same group from situation to situation. Such variants are known as markers. It is also possible to find examples of gradient stratification, in which there are obvious differences between different social groups, but these differences remain relatively stable from one situation to another. These variants are known as indicators.

Block One features appear to function as indicators. They show least stylistic variation and occur even in the most formal speech of a high proportion of speakers. Block Two features, in contrast, function as markers. There is a sharp stratification between situations 1, 2 and 3, on the one hand and situations 4 and 5, on the other hand. The differences between the features in the two blocks can be represented most clearly by plotting the typical patterns. For purposes of clarity, values for just two examples — dentals (from Block One) and the first person singular pronoun (from Block Two) — are plotted.

FIGURE 8 *Proportions of Speakers using Patois Variants of Dentals and First Person Singular Pronouns Situation by Situation*

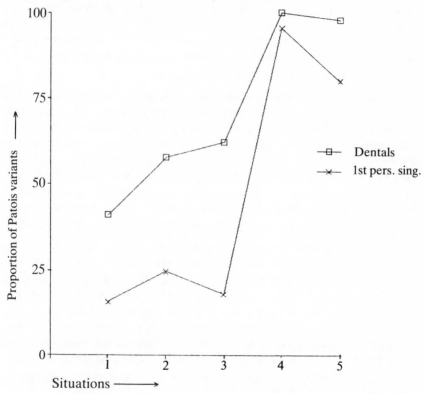

It is interesting to note that with the exception of some six speakers who used very high proportions of Patois throughout recording, no speaker used Block Two features in either of the situations which included a white participant. The same is true of situation 2, the formal black interview, except for the use of *mi*: some three speakers, in addition to the group of heavy Patois users, made limited use of this feature when talking to the black interviewer, presumably as a means of asserting ethnic solidarity. It seems reasonable to conclude that the presence of Block Two features represents a conscious marking of Patois. It was therefore used as the criterion for the definition of a situation as Patois or English.

Patterns of language choice

It has been pointed out already that many speakers completely, or almost completely, monitored out Patois features of phonology, morphology and syntax from certain situations so that their speech was indistinguishable, or virtually indistinguishable, from the local white norm. A highly focussed "English" variety was thus part of the linguistic repertoire of by far the largest proportion of the speakers in the sample. This English variety was most likely to occur in the formal white interview. It also characterized many of the black formal interviews and informal racially mixed conversations. It occurred very infrequently in black informal conversation and never when friends were left alone without the presence of an "outsider".

Whereas the use of English was often sustained throughout a situation, the same could not be said for the speakers' use of Patois. Only a very small proportion of speakers consistently used Patois, and even then they used it only in certain situations. Most of the recording was characterized by switching between "Patois" and "English", the relative proportions of the two varieties varying a great deal from speaker to speaker and situation to situation (see Chapter 3 for more detailed discussion). The situations which from this point on will be called "Patois" should thus be understood to refer in the main to code-switching behaviour between Patois and English varieties.

One of the most interesting features of language choice is the very definite patterning which emerged across the sample. The five different situations included in recordings could potentially throw up nine permutations of Patois and English usage. In actual fact we find just five different patterns: Patois usage in only one situation (always the black peer group situation); in two situations (always the peer group situation and the black informal conversation); in three situations (always the peer group and black informal conversations and the black formal interview), in four situations (always the three black situations and the informal racially mixed

TABLE 10 *Patterns of Language Use*

	No. of speakers	Situation 1 (white formal)	Situation 3 (white informal)	Situation 2 (black formal)	Situation 5 (black informal)	Situation 4 (black peers)
Pattern 1	5	English	English	English	English	Patois
Pattern 2	14	English	English	English	Patois	Patois
Pattern 3	13	English	English	Patois	Patois	Patois
Pattern 4	4	English	Patois	Patois	Patois	Patois
Pattern 5	6	Patois	Patois	Patois	Patois	Patois

conversation); and in all five situations. The implicational relationships which emerge can be seen clearly in Table 10 opposite.

It was clearly important to examine the symbolic significance of different patterns of language choice and to establish whether speakers who made the same choices would also share non-linguistic characteristics.

The relationship between language patterns and other measures

There is, inevitably, a relationship between the Patois patterns and the various other measures which we have already discussed. Thus, any speaker who achieves a low frequency score is likely to use Patois in a large number of situations. By the same token, it seems reasonable to assume that a speaker with a high competence score (see Chapter 8) is more likely to use Patois features in a wide range of situations than one with a low competence score. It is important to note, however, the potential independence of these measures. For most patterns, there is a range of frequency scores rather than a cluster of scores around the same point. Pattern scores therefore allow us to measure individual adaptations to situation and recognize that, for different speakers, different degrees of Patois usage can signal the same conversational intent.

Table 11 shows that it is possible to make a number of valid generalizations for speakers who exhibit Pattern One, Four and Five behaviour. For instance, Pattern One speakers are likely to have limited competence in Patois and to use Patois features very infrequently. Pattern Four and Five speakers, in contrast, are likely to be extremely competent Patois speakers who use Patois features frequently. However, it is not possible to make the same kind of prediction about the young people who exhibit Pattern Two and Three behaviour. Although Pattern Three speakers tend to be more competent as a group and to use Patois features more frequently than Pattern Two speakers, there is a very wide range of competence and frequency scores for both patterns. Almost 70% of the sample follow one of these two patterns. Language patterns thus allow us to make further inter-individual distinctions which may shed light on the mechanisms and motivation for language choice.

The same explanatory variables considered in the analysis of frequency and competence scores — sex, education, network and acquiescence–criticalness — were used in relation to pattern scores. Only network was found to have a statistically significant effect on the Patois pattern scores (significant level: >1%). However, whilst education and acquiescence–criticalness did not achieve statistical significance, a number of observations can be made. If we consider first education, we find that it is possible to

TABLE 11 *Distribution of Frequency and Competence Scores according to Language Pattern*

Speaker Number	Pattern	Competence Score	Frequency Score	Frequency Range
20	1	9	93.50	
21	1	10	94.38	
27	1	10	93.59	91.56 to 96.17
35	1	11	96.17	
26	1	12	91.56	
37	2	8	96.29	
39	2	9	94.94	
36	2	10	96.17	
17	2	11	88.08	
38	2	12	92.87	
26	2	13	92.45	
3	2	14	88.99	81.49 to 96.29
8	2	14	88.60	
10	2	14	86.00	
19	2	14	90.93	
42	2	16	81.49	
31	2	18	88.37	
18	2	20	81.73	
41	2	20	83.46	
1	3	13	79.77	
2	3	13	89.77	
9	3	14	88.90	
14	3	15	89.59	
6	3	15	89.17	
7	3	17	91.95	
13	3	18	82.93	78.5 to 91.95
4	3	19	90.26	
11	3	19	89.43	
12	3	19	78.81	
15	3	19	79.20	
34	3	19	86.88	
29	3	20	78.53	
28	4	17	78.39	
24	4	19	42.63	42.63 to 78.39
23	4	20	63.62	
40	4	20	67.50	
32	5	18	37.61	
45	5	18	29.34	
16	5	20	71.32	29.34 to 71.32
33	5	20	48.99	
43	5	20	40.39	
44	5	20	34.10	

TABLE 12 *Distribution of Education Scores According to Language Pattern*

Speaker Number	Pattern	Education Score
26	1	10
27	1	9
35	1	6
20	1	6
21	1	4
39	2	10
38	2	9
26	2	9
8	2	8
31	2	8
37	2	7
17	2	6
41	2	6
42	2	6
10	2	5
3	2	4
19	2	4
18	2	1
36	2	0
11	3	10
9	3	9
6	3	9
34	3	7
1	3	6
7	3	6
14	3	6
2	3	5
4	3	5
12	3	4
13	3	4
15	3	1
30	3	1
29	3	0
23	4	1
24	4	1
28	4	1
40	4	1
33	5	4
45	5	4
44	5	3
16	5	2
43	5	1
32	5	0

made generalizations similar to those in the discussion of the distribution of competence and frequency scores above.

Thus, Pattern One speakers are likely to perform well in school, to be female and to have high educational aspirations, whilst Pattern Four and Five speakers are likely to be male and educational underachievers. No such predictions, however, can be made for Pattern Two and Three speakers, since a wide spread of education scores is to be found in each of these groups.

A somewhat different picture emerges for the distribution of scores of acquiescence–criticalness, which can be best illustrated by a discussion of the range of scores within each pattern.

TABLE 13 *Range of Acquiescence–Criticalness Scores for each Language Pattern*

Pattern	No. of Speakers	Acquiescence–Criticalness
1	5	−1 to +3
2	14	−6 to +5
3	13	−7 to +7
4	4	0 to +3
5	6	−2 to −7

Patterns One to Three are unremarkable. Again, there is clearly no relationship between Patterns Two and Three and scores of acquiescence–criticalness. The narrower range for Pattern One speakers may well be a function of the smaller sample size. However, a very surprising picture emerges for Pattern Four and Five speakers. In previous discussions, Pattern Four and Five speakers have tended to exhibit similar behaviour, but now their acquiescence–criticalness scores sharply diverge. Whereas Pattern Five speakers have consistently negative acquiescence–criticalness scores, Pattern Four speakers have consistently positive scores. It may be possible, for instance, that Pattern Four speakers' relatively favourable attitudes towards white mainstream society influence them to use "English" rather than "Patois" in the formal white interview. Again, this finding may well be a function of the small sample sizes and therefore needs to be interpreted with caution. It is possible, however, that this apparent discrepancy may give important clues as to the motivation for language choice.

Motivation for language choice

Any discussion of the motivation for language choice in a British Black community will necessarily be on two levels. The first level affects the marking of a situation as either "English" or "Patois". It should be remembered, however, that the linguistic opposition we are considering is not in fact a direct opposition between English and Patois, since the Patois situations most frequently involve code-switching behaviour between Patois and English. The second level thus concerns this code-switching behaviour. The mechanisms which underlie switching are of central importance for our understanding of the linguistic behaviour of British-born black people.

The quite distinct patterns of language use which emerge from the data, however, make it possible to consider these two levels of language choice separately. By far the largest proportion of the sample exhibit distinctly bi-dialectal behaviour, using exclusively or almost exclusively English variants in some situations and introducing Patois features only in certain others. Thus, although a description of intra-situational code-switching behaviour is of considerable interest (and forms the focus for Sebba, 1984a, b, c, in press; and Sutcliffe, forthcoming), inter-situational language choice is of complementary importance.

Various theoretical and pre-theoretical frameworks have been proposed for the explanation of language choice. Giles' (1973, 1977) theory of Speech Accommodation, for instance, is concerned with the motivations and social consequences which underlie changes in people's speech styles. It suggests that people modify — or accommodate — their speech in a way which takes into consideration the speech of other participants in a conversation. Depending on their perceptions of the interactive situation, they can either shift their speech style towards (speech convergence) or away from (speech divergence) the speech style of their interlocutors. Speech convergence reduces the linguistic (and hence social) differences between speakers and is motivated by the desire to express or receive approval. Similarly, speech divergence serves to accentuate these differences and can be used to communicate disapproval.

The empirical evidence for speech accommodation comes from a wide range of linguistic features, including accent (Giles, 1973), speech rate (Matarazzo, 1973), vocal intensity (Natalé, 1975) and language choice (Giles, Taylor & Bourhis, 1973). There is also evidence of the particular relevance of speech divergence in asserting ethnic identity in inter-group relations (Bourhis & Giles, 1977; Bourhis, Giles, Leyens & Tajfel, 1979) and their attitudes towards the other participants.

An obvious determinant of the individual's behaviour in inter-ethnic situations is the status and prestige which is afforded to a given language variety within a community. Again, Giles and colleagues (Giles, Bourhis & Taylor, 1977) have made important contributions to the discussion of this general area. They propose that the influence of social factors on inter-ethnic communication can be described in terms of "ethnolinguistic vitality" which is defined by structural characteristics such as status, demography and institutional support. In a given community, the language with the strongest ethnolinguistic vitality would be expected to predominate. Thus, in a British context, the number of standard speakers greatly exceeds the number of Patois speakers, and standard English is the language of education and other important institutions whereas Patois has no official status. The notion of ethnolinguistic vitality predicts that minority and majority groups will recognize the prestige of standard English and devalue Patois, a prediction which adequately describes the group reaction (see Chapter 3), but makes no allowance for individual departures from agreed social norms or the significance of such departures.

Scotton (1980) goes a step further by taking into account both the interactional dynamics which form the substance of accommodation theory and the societal norms implicit in the notion of ethnolinguistic vitality. She proposes that linguistic choices are individually motivated negotiations of identity. When a role relationship between participants is well defined, there will be general agreement as to the *unmarked* linguistic choice for each side. If speakers choose to use the unmarked code, they are identifying with the status associated with their role relationship. If, however, speakers choose the *marked* variety, they are clearly rejecting the status implied by the role relationship. If a role relationship is weakly defined, a series of exploratory choices will be made to identify the type of role relationship and the speaker's identity within it. She proposes a set of hypotheses (Scotton, 1980: 362–63) regarding the frequency of types of choices and the factors with which they are most closely associated. The first hypothesis states that:

"(1) In well-defined role relationships in which a power differential is a factor in status identification, unmarked choices will dominate. In such relationships, code selection can best be predicted in terms of salient group identities of the participants and other situational factors."

In terms of British Black speech data, it is quite clear that English is the unmarked choice for the formal interviews with both black and white researchers. The situation with the white interviewer is the most straightforward. Only six speakers make the marked choice and use Patois while responding to formal questions. Those who follow this course are minimizing the social distance and are rejecting the inferior status associated with Patois within the role relationship. By failing to observe widely agreed upon social norms for this kind of interaction, they are making statements not only about the immediate communication but about their attitudes towards the dominant society as a whole, which are understood by black and white participants alike.

Scotton's second hypothesis states:

"(2) In well-defined role relationships in which a power differential is a factor in status-identification, marked choices may occur depending on the dynamics and content of the interaction. Marked choices will occur with a higher frequency in these relationships than in those in which a power differential is a factor."

Again, patterns of language choice in young British Black speakers support this hypothesis. Almost half the speakers marked the formal black interview as Patois. Clearly, considerable confusion existed in speakers' minds. On the one hand, the situation was formal and the role relationships were well-defined. On the other hand, the most powerful person in the inter-action was black, a very unusual event for most British Blacks beyond the immediate confines of the black community. For half of the sample, the solidarity motif was stronger than the power differential.

This can be seen more clearly when we examine the next interaction between speakers and the black fieldworker. The formal stance of the interviewer is abandoned, food and drinks are passed around and there is a free exchange of opinions on a wide range of subjects. Forty out of 45 speakers make the marked choice in this situation, confirming Scotton's hypothesis that marked choices will occur more frequently in relationships where power differential is an incidental in status identification.

Scotton's third and final hypothesis states that:

"(3) In weakly defined role relationships, which particular ex-ploratory choices are presented for unmarked status will depend on the nature of the goals participants have for the relationship. For example, whether they have long or short term goals for the duration of the relationship is a potential independent variable. Individual personality characteristics, including goals, will be better predictors of linguistic choices than are group identities or situational factors."

Again, patterns of language choice in young British Black speakers support this hypothesis. Like the formal black interview, the informal racially mixed conversation is a little ambiguous. The young white fieldworker is presented as somebody who is helping, but not part of the project proper. He is young, friendly and interested and makes efforts to minimize the social distance between himself and other participants in the conversation. This role rela-tionship is thus a good deal more weakly defined than that of the interviewer–

subject. This is reflected to some extent by the fact that four more speakers made a marked linguistic choice in this situation than in the formal interview. The majority of young people, however, chose the unmarked variety in this situation. This choice is no doubt a function between the speakers. There are reports of Patois usage in inter-racial situations (cf. Hewitt, 1982), but presumably this usage is a function of intimacy and not simply status.

Community views on patterns of language choice

Self-reports of language use can be notoriously unreliable (cf. Labov, 1966; V. Edwards, 1979; Teitelbaum, 1979; Chapter 3 of this book) and freely expressed opinions on language use should not necessarily be accepted at face value, particularly when dealing with low status varieties. However, it is often possible to gain a great deal of insight by listening carefully to speakers' views on, and feelings about their own language. Certainly the young people in the present sample showed great sensitivity to the social motivation for different kinds of language behaviour and their views on the symbolic functions of Patois usage lend support to the analysis offered in the present chapter.

By far the majority of British Black people can and do use "English", recognize its importance and therefore have at least partially fulfilled their parents' hopes (see Chapter 8). Young people talked in terms of speaking English in order to get jobs, to be understood and to show that you are "somebody worth dealing with". Continued facility in Patois in the face of opposition from both mainstream white society and parents may therefore be perceived as both perverse and bizarre by teachers and other "outsiders". Speakers' own reflections on this subject, however, leave no doubt as to the underlying rationale for such patterns of language behaviour. They paint a clear picture of the kind of conscious choices which people have to make:

> **Polly:** When Jackie talks to anybody she just talks in the same way
> so therefore they say she can't speak English. She *can* speak
> English, but . . .
> **Marie:** She can but she don't want to.

The most significant single use of Patois would seem to be the signalling of a group identity. This can be done, as in Jackie's case, by using Patois features in all situations. It can also be done by restricting Patois to more intimate black peer group situations. Those young people, however, who choose to use English in conversations in which Patois is generally considered to be more appropriate are often the objects of criticism and scorn. Nora, for instance, was incensed by her sister's behaviour:

"My sister, she's a right little snobby . . . if she came here now she'd speak plain English, but she can speak Patois better than me. She speaks it to me, to some of her coloured friends who she knows speak Patois, but to her snobby coloured friends she speaks English. She talks Queen English, brebber. She's the snotty one of the family."

There was a keen awareness of the power and force associated with Patois and the effect which this can sometimes have on white people:

"It terrify white people cos they don't know what you're saying and if they do know what you're saying, dem know that it bad because it's a very expressive language."

Sometimes Patois usage can exclude outsiders. It is a very effective medium for jokes about people who are not a part of the group. It is also a private language which allows blacks to talk about non-blacks without being understood. In this way it underlines the "them" and "us" dimensions of intergroup relations. It can also be used to express contempt. Frequent reference was made to the role of Patois in "cussing" and other expressions of anger. Several young people described its use in a school setting as a means of expressing defiance of teachers. This was usually a source of considerable humour.

Ray: Mi used to use Patois a lot, you know and just cuss dem.

James: You go, "You blood clart!" and the teacher goes "What did you say?"

Ray: "I know what that was, I know what that was" and all dat, dat time dem no know what you say. Dem say "You say bastard" and all dis.

James: Yea, dem say, you swear, they say, "Well you did swear, didn't you? Go to the headmaster," or some daftness like that.

Ray: And di headmaster say, "What did you say?" You no go say to di headmaster seh you say blood clart, you say, "I said 'baby'" or something like that.

Patois and white people

Hewitt (1982) draws attention to the role which Patois plays in the politics of friendship between black and white adolescents. His work is based on observation and discussion in mixed youth clubs in South London where many white members showed varying degrees of Patois usage. Sometimes this usage was limited to certain set phrases; sometimes it extended to sustained Patois conversations. The use of Patois in these settings signals the acceptance of black friends and the desire to be accepted. However, given the central importance of Patois in the marking of a separate black identity, the use of Patois by white speakers is bound to set up certain tensions in young black people. As Hewitt points out, the only way in which white youths can successfully acquire Patois is with the participation and encouragement of the black peers. However, the most common reaction of young black people is hostility.

Remarks made by participants in the present study indicated that Patois usage by whites, and indeed other ethnic groups, was a rare but well-known phenomenon and that it sometimes extended beyond adolesence. Reactions varied between appreciation:

> "This woman up the road she can chat, she can chat. Lord have mercy . . . if you heard her you wouldn't think she was white!"

> "With this guy I know you could throw anything at him and he'd understand . . . I didn't have to change down for him."

> "I heard this Indian in the Wednesday market. I heard him talk Patois and he talks it ever so good."

and scathing criticism:

> "I don't think Indians should be speaking Patois."

> "It's the white girls that make me sick."

> "Everybody should stick to their own grounds."

> "I don't like it, I don't like it. It doesn't blend."

> "Some of the English people are trying to speak Patois and I hate that. It's nothing to do with them. Patois doesn't come naturally to them, so they should stick to their own language and stop talking ours."

> "They use all these bad words and they use them and they don't know what they mean."

Young British Black people thus show a keen awareness of two main symbolic functions of Patois usage. First, it is used to mark ethnic solidarity. On the one hand, it can serve to show the speaker's desire to identify with black culture and values; on the other hand, its use can indicate that the person being addressed is felt to be a member of the group. Second, it can be used to indicate rejection by the speaker of the accepted norms for interaction. If Patois is used in a situation where the consensus view would suggest that English is appropriate, then the intention is clearly to show contempt for the low status ascribed to black language and culture by white mainstream society. It can also be used to exclude outsiders from the group.

Summary

Having considered the social correlates of both different frequencies of Patois usage (Chapter 7) and different levels of competence (Chapter 8), the present chapter concentrates on the different patterns of Patois usage across the sample. One of the major problems in describing any patterns which might exist was deciding what actually constitutes Patois usage. Close examination of the data revealed that only a small number of Patois features (the phonological variants, and uninflected plurals and present tense verbs) were found in those situations which emerged from the quantitative analysis in Chapter 7 as most English. The more Patois situations contained both these features (labelled Block One) and a wide range of other Patois variants (labelled Block Two). This provided an objective criterion for the classification of a situation as "Patois" or "English": the presence of Block Two features was held to mark a situation as "Patois".

This system of classification allowed us to identify five quite distinct patterns of language choice: Patois only in the black peer group situation (Pattern One); Patois in the two informal black situations (Pattern Two); Patois in all three black situations (Pattern Three); Patois in all situations except the formal white interview (Pattern Four); and Patois in all five situations (Pattern Five). Social network was found to have a statistically significant effect on language patterns. The relationships between language patterns and education and acquiescence–criticalness, the two other explanatory variables which have previously been considered, were more complex. Pattern One speakers were associated with high achievers; Pattern Four and Five speakers tended to be low achievers; but Patterns Two and Three were found to be poor predictors of education. A similar range of attitudes towards mainstream white society was to be found for all patterns, though it is speculated that the fact that Pattern Four speakers were rather less critical than Pattern Five speakers may account for the fact that they chose to use English in the formal white interview.

The symbolic significance of language choice is discussed. Patois is associated with a group identity: it can be used to signal solidarity and exclude outsiders. It is suggested that there is concensus within a community as to which language variety is the unmarked choice in any given situation. If individuals then use the marked variety, it is likely to be perceived as an aggressive assertion of the minority group identity, and a refusal to accept the low status assigned to that group by the dominant society. The main insight offered by an analysis in terms of language patterns is realization that the same conversational intent can be conveyed both by highly competent and by less competent Patois speakers.

10 Conclusions

We started with a number of questions which, prior to the present study, were either the subject of speculation or had given rise to conflicting answers. The first of these questions concerned the proportion of young British Blacks who regularly used Patois in certain situations. Some writers (e.g. Rosen & Burgess, 1980) claimed that as few as 10 to 20% of black children fell into this category; others (e.g. Hadi, 1976; Sutcliffe, 1982a) estimated that between 70 and 80% regularly used Patois. One writer (Tomlin, 1981) reported that 100% of her random sample claimed they spoke Patois.

Another question of concern was the social constraints on language use. It has been proposed, for instance, that the young people who take pride in "talking black" are those who have chosen a life style associated with the black youth culture which revolves around reggae and other specifically black forms of music and dance (cf. Crump, 1979). Patois usage is thus seen as a conscious assertion of black identity and a reflection of hostility towards mainstream white society. However, this is the only potential social determinant of language behaviour which has received attention, and for this reason it was felt important to consider a range of other variables, including the sex, education and network relations of speakers.

The question of fluency or competence in Patois was also considered. This is an area which has been extremely difficult to define. It is tempting, for instance, to assume that those young black people who use Patois in a wide range of situations are those who are most competent in Patois, and that those who do not use Patois in racially mixed situations like school are not in fact able to do so. However, it does not necessarily follow that children who choose to use English in conversations with white people, cannot use Patois in other situations.

A related issue concerns the definition of a situation as "English" or "Patois". We know that we are likely to find a range of Patois competence in the black community. We also know that black peer group speech is often characterized by rapid switching between Patois and English variants. But, given the likely nature and extent of variation between and within individual speakers, is it possible or feasible, to make a division between "English" and "Patois" situations? If so, would such a division enable us to go beyond measures of frequency to examine the actual patterns of language use which may exist and the social significance attached to them?

Methodological implications of the study

The most important prerequisite for an understanding of questions of the kind outlined above is an adequate corpus of data. Such a corpus would need to accurately reflect both individual variation and as wide a range as possible of the linguistic repertoires which are to be found within the British Black community. It should also include detailed information on the social characteristics of the speakers which would permit an explanation for any patterns of linguistic behaviour which may be observed. The collection of data which meet these requirements, however, poses many challenges for the linguist.

In monolingual communities like Lower East Side New York (cf. Labov, 1966) or Norwich (Trudgill, 1974), it was possible to supplement more formal styles with casual speech by asking speakers to tell a humorous or dramatic story. The usefulness of this technique, however, would appear to vary from one situation to another. Gal (1979), for instance, reports that invitations to tell stories did not succeed in producing changes in style or language choice in Austrian–Hungarian bilinguals, and our own experience of British black speakers (V. Edwards, 1979; Sutcliffe, 1982a) supports this observation. An obvious explanation for the failure of this technique in a British situation might be in terms of the ethnicity of the interviewer. If Patois usage is usually associated with "black" conversation, the invitation to tell a story will predictably provoke an English rather than a Patois response. It is interesting to note, however, that ethnicity is not the only factor. Attempts to elicit Patois in this way by a black interviewer as part of early formulations of fieldwork for the present study were only marginally more successful. It would appear that once a situation has been defined as formal by black speakers, the story telling technique is not powerful enough to override formality constraints.

For this reason, it was decided to build into recordings a credible — and quite genuine — reason for leaving speakers alone. Young people were told that we wanted to find out their views on a wide range of issues of interest to the black community and were asked to complete a questionnaire. It was explained that they would be left alone so that they would not feel inhibited by the presence of an outsider, and they were encouraged to discuss the answers among themselves. The questionnaire contained references to the police, teachers, language and other issues, which in our experience, frequently give rise to Patois usage.

The technique of leaving speakers on their own has been used successfully before by Sutcliffe (1982a) and, more recently, by Sebba (1984a, b, c, in press). The present formulation, however, has a number of advantages over previous ones. The practice of recording people without their knowledge obviously raises ethical problems. However, the very fact of seeking permission limits the range of speakers who will actually take part. It is likely that those who equate Patois with very private black interaction will either refuse to take part or carefully monitor the language behaviour throughout recording, irrespective of whether or not the researcher is present. Speakers who feel insecure about their competence in Patois may also be reluctant to take part in an exercise of this kind. The range of speakers for whom this technique is useful may thus necessarily be limited.

In the present project, no attempt was made to conceal the fact that speakers were being recorded. However, by situating the black peer group conversation towards the end of the session, and by offering a genuinely absorbing activity, speakers indicated by their linguistic behaviour and in comments made at the end of recording that they had either forgotten or were not worried about the presence of the tape recorder. This format also has the advantage of more or less standardizing the subjects of conversation and providing a much more realistic basis for comparison than would have been the case in free recordings. It allowed us to collect all the data in one session, and thus by-pass the problems of trying to locate speakers on a number of different occasions. A further off-shoot of this technique was that we were able to collect a wide range of information on participants' social characteristics, including their attitudes and network relations.

Social network as an analytical tool

The importance of social networks for an understanding of black language usage cannot be overestimated. More traditionally, sociolinguistic studies have made use of social class divisions in the analysis of linguistic variation. In ethnically homogeneous monolingual communities like Norwich and Lower East Side New York, it would appear that social class is a good predictor of a wide range of other variables, including level of education and behaviour. In other words, social class groupings based on occupational status, are culturally relevant for these communities.

There is every reason to suppose, however, that the cultural relevance of social class varies considerably from one community to another. Its usefulness in peasant and non-industrialized societies has been questioned, for instance, by Gal (1979) in Europe, by Bortoni de Figueiredo Ricardo (1983) in Brazil and by Russell (1982) in Africa. Certainly, in a British context, job levels are often poor indicators of level of education (cf. Troyna & Smith, 1983), and it is doubtful if the generalizations about social class can be applied in the same way to black and white populations in Britain.

Social network has the advantage of allowing gradient classification rather than the imposition of strict categories. A network approach makes it possible to consider individual speakers in relation to the communities in which they operate in ways which are beyond the grasp of a group analysis. Most important it provides an explanatory mechanism for any differences which emerge, by recognizing the normative influence of social networks on the language use of their members. It may be interesting, for instance, to discover that certain kinds of linguistic behaviour are correlated with lower middle class speakers (cf. Labov, 1966; Trudgill, 1974). However, such findings tell us nothing of the reasons why this should be the case. The same observation applies to some of the other variables, including sex of speaker, which have been used in sociolinguistic studies. Network analysis takes us beyond mere correlations to an understanding of the processes which mediate linguistic variation.

Network analysis falls more within the tradition of social anthropology than other branches of sociology. However, the decision to undertake a network analysis of the present data takes into account the differences of opinion currently to be found among British sociologists of race. Many observers have attempted to segment the diversity which exists within the British Black community in terms of an analysis of lifestyles. It is easy to understand the attractions of this approach for a community which includes groups like Rastafarians and Pentecostal Christians, differentiated not only by their philosophies but by physical appearance and dress. Serious objections, however, have been raised to such attempts (see, for instance, Figueroa, 1982) on the grounds that they trivialize the extent of this diversity and sometimes give undue emphasis to numerically small groups in a way which helps to perpetuate stereotypical views of black people. A network study by-passes these objections by basing its analysis on the individual rather than pre-determined groups.

Implications of the findings for knowledge of black language in Britain

Our conclusions are based on the careful analysis of the speech of some 45 young British Black people in Dudley, West Midlands. They were selected to represent a range of social characteristics identified through close ethnographic observation as likely to influence linguistic behaviour. This approach is very different from one which aims to locate and study the language of a random, representative sample. The absence of any ready-made sampling frame rules out the possibility of working with a representative sample. Census data contain no information on ethnicity, and other methods used in identifying linguistic minorities (cf. G. Smith, 1984) such as name analysis, or consulting community lists, are not feasible in the case of the British Black community. The non-random distribution of black people, both geographically and across the generally accepted socio-economic groupings (see Chapter 5), also makes random sampling impractical.

However, while noting that it was simply not possible to consider random sampling for the present study, it should be remembered that the "judgement" or "quota" sample which was actually chosen is far more appropriate for a study which aims to explore the relationships between language use and social factors. While we cannot claim representativeness either for the black population of Dudley or British Black people nationally, our findings confirm, modify or refute our initial hypotheses about the relations between language use and the social characteristics of the speaker. The striking patterns which emerge from the data strongly suggest that our conclusions are valid for Dudley. Further studies may well demonstrate that they are also valid for the wider British Black community.

In order to characterize the language behaviour of young British born black people, it is necessary to examine a number of different aspects of that behaviour. Three main questions have been addressed. First, are there differences in the overall frequency with which speakers use Patois variants? If so, is it possible to identify the social and stylistic factors which affect this variation? Second, are all members of the British Black community equally competent in the use of Patois? If not, what range of competence exists and what social factors are associated with different degrees of competence? Third, is it possible to discern different patterns of Patois usage which would enable us to explain the symbolic functions of "English" and "Patois" usage?

Patois frequency

The relative proportions of Patois and English variants of some 11 commonly occurring features were calculated for each speaker in each of the five different situations included in recording. By further calculating the mean of these frequencies, it was possible to construct Patois *index scores* which could be used to examine the effect of ethnicity and formality on Patois usage.

In spite of considerable inter-individual differences, a very definite pattern emerged. Three situations were perceived as more "English": the interviews with the black and white researchers and the informal racially mixed conversation. Two situations emerged as less "English": the black peer group conversation and the informal conversation with the black researcher. The interview with the white researcher emerged as the most "English" of all the situations. Speakers varied, however, in their perceptions of the other two situations: some considered the black formal interview to be more "English"; others used more "English" speech patterns for the informal racially mixed conversation.

In considering possible explanations for different frequencies of Patois usage, it was more feasible to correlate background variables with one measure rather than five different index scores. A *frequency score*, based on the mean of the five index scores, was therefore calculated for each speaker. Statistically significant relationships were found between frequency scores and three different explanatory variables: network relations, the interaction of education and sex; and attitudes towards mainstream white society. The more integrated into the black community, the more frequent the use of Patois is likely to be. Similarly, the more critical the speakers towards mainstream white society, the greater the use of Patois variants. In the present sample, education appeared to decrease the frequency of Patois usage in young men, but to have no effect on the speech of the young women. The number of underachieving women included in the study, however, was very small and a sample more equally balanced for educational achievement and aspirations might have shown men and women behaving in a similar way.

Patois competence

"Patois" is a convenient label for a very wide range of actual usage. For some speakers, it involves the use of certain phonological variants, some distinctively Patois words and phrases, and a small number of stereotypically Patois grammatical features, such as pronouns and uninflected verbs and nouns. For others, it entails not only Patois phonology and vocabulary but the full range of grammatical features normally associated with Jamaican Creole.

It is very obvious that Patois features are acquired in a set order and not distributed at random among speakers. There is evidence of a pattern very similar to that which has been shown to hold for learners of English as a second language. Features are not acquired individually but in groups, and it is possible to demonstrate several acquisitional hierarchies. Implicational relations can be shown to hold between these hierarchies in such a way that speakers who regularly use features belonging to one group will also use those features in all the groups below. Acquisitional hierachies also allow us to distinguish between speakers. Almost 40% of participants in the study were able to use all five groups of features, some 5% used only Group One features consistently; while the rest of the young people were distributed between these two extremes.

There is thus considerable variation in the Patois competence of the speakers, as measured by their use of a wide range of features. A statistically significant relationship was found to hold between the level of competence and the network relations of the speaker. It would appear that the more integrated into the black community a speaker, the more competent the level of Patois. Although all black children have the opportunity to hear Patois from parents, there is an expectation that they should not use it themselves with their elders. The presence of strong black peer network relations is therefore a prerequisite for competence in Patois.

It is also interesting to note that level of education and attitudes towards mainstream white society do not in themselves have a significant effect on the speakers' level of competence. Several of the young people who had done well at school proved to be highly competent Patois speakers, as did several of those who showed very little hostility towards mainstream white society. The stereotype of the disaffected low-achieving male Patois user thus bears little relationship to the patterns which emerged in the discussion of competence.

Patterns of Patois usage

Given the range of Patois features which exists in the speech of British Black people, and the different levels of competence, there is clearly some difficulty in deciding what precisely constitutes Patois usage. It would not be desirable, for instance, to label a situation as "Patois" simply on the basis of the occasional substitution of a Patois vowel variant for an English one. The division into more and less English situations which emerged in the consideration of Patois index scores, however, gives valuable indications of ways in which objective decisions can be made as to whether a situation should be interpreted as "English" or "Patois".

With the exception of a small number of individuals who used high proportions of Patois in all five situations, close examination of the English behaviour of other participants in the three most English situations showed some interesting consistencies. Many of these speakers used no Patois variants at all in the English situations; those who did use Patois variants used only a very narrow range, which included the phonological features, uninflected plurals and third person singular present tense verbs. On this basis, the features which made up the Patois index were divided into two different blocks: those which marked a situation as Patois and those which did not.

This distinction allowed an objective classification into "English" and "Patois" for all speakers in all situations. The patterns which emerged were extremely revealing. Although there were nine possible permutations of language choice for the five situations, only five different combinations actually emerged: Patois in all five situations; Patois in all situations except the formal white interview; Patois in all three black situations; Patois in only the two informal black situations; and Patois only in the black peer group situation. The pattern score for each speaker was correlated with the various background variables and, again, there was found to be a statistically significant relationship between the patterns of speakers' language use and their network relations.

One of the most interesting findings which emerges in the discussion of pattern scores is that different ranges of Patois features can serve exactly the same symbolic function for different speakers. A highly competent speaker will mark a situation as black with a wide range of features; a less competent speaker will make use of a much more limited range. This finding would seem to explain, in part at least, the astounding differences between researchers' estimates of Patois usage.

The effect on other participants in the conversation, black or white, of different ranges of Patois usage is likely to be the same. In a situation where English would be the unmarked or expected choice, the use of Patois signals a refusal to comply with the social status ascribed to the two varieties by the majority group. It is a powerful assertion of black identity, and may be perceived as threatening and disconcerting by white participants in an exchange. In situations where Patois is the consensus choice, the use of Patois communicates warmth, friendship and solidarity. It can also sometimes be used very effectively for excluding white people from the conversation. Conversely, the use of English in these situations indicates racial aloofness and is likely to be interpreted as "snobby" or "prissy".

Implications of the findings for teachers

It is widely assumed in educational circles that Patois is no longer an important social force in the lives of British Black people. It would appear, however, that many observers have quite simply been asking the wrong questions. It is more informative, for instance, to ask what range of competence in Patois exists within the British Black community than what proportion of young black people speak Patois. Agreement on what constitutes Patois usage is critical and confusion surrounding this issue has no doubt been responsible, in part at least, for the very large differences in estimates of how many young black people speak Patois. A little over one third of the speakers in the present sample would be described as Patois speakers if we used the full range of Jamaican Creole as the criterion for such a decision. However, if we define Patois in such a way as to include speakers who use a narrower range of features, generally agreed to "mark" a situation as Patois, then all of the young people in the study can be considered Patois speakers. It has been argued that it is more illuminating to accept the latter definition rather than the former. In spite of the variations in competence between speakers, it allows for a unified explanation of the symbolic role of Patois in the British Black community.

Other aspects of conventional wisdom have also been thrown into question by the findings of the study. It is commonly assumed, for instance, that Patois usage is associated with a strong assertion of black identity and expressions of hostility to mainstream white society. While the present analysis confirms this largely commonsense position, it also shows that this is only a very partial explanation for British Black language use. Attitudes towards white society affect the frequency with which speakers use Patois features, but do not necessarily reflect the level of Patois competence. And variables such as network relations have been shown to exert a statistically significant effect on all measures of language behaviour.

Information about the patterns and range of Patois usage among British Blacks is important to teachers for a number of reasons. For instance, teachers need to appreciate the symbolic functions of Patois if they are able to fully understand the black pupils in their care. The deliberate use of Patois in formal situations can be an act of defiance, a statement that speakers do not accept the low status which white society attaches to black people and their characteristic forms of speech. Patois usage does not in any way indicate low ability, or the need for some kind of remedial intervention on the part of the teacher. It would be equally misguided to assume that because speakers show no evidence of black language use in school they cannot and do not speak Patois in other settings. Although the actual competence of the speakers in the sample varied a great deal, all used Patois features to signal friendship and solidarity.

It is also important for teachers to understand the ambivalent attitudes towards language which characterize not only British Black people but all speakers of low status varieties. While the prestige of the high status variety is recognized by all, it sometimes carries connotations of prissiness and insincerity (cf. Giles & Powesland, 1975). The low status variety, in contrast, is associated with trustworthiness and warmth. Any attempt to discuss low status language with its speakers needs to be interpreted through this matrix. Teachers should not be surprised by the reluctance of children to admit to using a stigmatized variety, given the range of negative connotations it evokes for the majority group. Neither should they be too quick to interpret this denial as evidence of low self-esteem. Language is a very private possession and attempts to intrude may well meet considerable and understandable resistance.

The use of Patois in the classroom has given rise to a great deal of controversy. Many teachers, often but not always white, argue strongly for its inclusion in the curriculum. Many parents and some sociologists counter that such initiatives are tokenist and doomed to failure. Stone (1981), for instance, applies Bourdieu's analysis to the British situation, suggesting that the introduction of Patois into schools is simply an attempt to defend the legitimate culture of the school against the "heretical" culture of black people. She argues that any attempts to "legitimize" Patois will result in the development of new varieties of Patois which serve the same functions as the present forms. Carby (1980) makes the equally pertinent observation that familiarity with dialect forms on the part of teachers will not remove the racist attitudes within the school and society at large which are the most serious obstacle to social equality for black people.

The findings of the present study can lend unequivocal support to neither position. It seems fairly clear that initiatives to introduce Patois into the school as a subject on the same level as other mother tongues would be doomed to failure. Unlike the South Asian and European linguistic minorities, the British Black community has never articulated any demands for mother tongue teaching. On the contrary, they have always firmly held the view that standard English is the only acceptable medium of education. However, attempts to introduce Patois have never been on this level.

Those who advocate the use of Patois, are usually exponents of a language awareness position (cf. Rosen & Burgess, 1980; V. Edwards, 1983). They argue that the linguistic diversity which exists within multicultural classrooms is a resource on which to build rather than a problem to overcome, and that all children are likely to gain in confidence and understanding by exploring — and sharing — their own language use. Patois is thus just one aspect of language study, and is considered in relation to the whole range of diversity in the school. Many myths and stereotypes about language abound in schools either as a result of overt statements or because of more subtle errors of omission. Although language awareness is not likely to substantially change the racist realities of society as a whole, it can nonetheless be seen as a useful element in anti-racist teaching.

Where next?

The present study has focussed on one British Black community. It can be supplemented to some extent by information on the black communities in Bedford (Sutcliffe, 1982a) and London (Sebba, in press; Sebba & Wootton, 1984). Direct comparisons, however, are not possible because of differences in methodology. We therefore have no clear information on any geographical variation which may exist. It is also notable that the communities on which these three studies have been based are very strongly Jamaican in origin. Sebba & Le Page (1983) suggest that the speech of young black people in London whose parents came from other islands also show strong Jamaican influence, but this is a question which remains to be studied systematically. It is also interesting to speculate what the situation would be in High Wycombe where the majority of the black population comes from St. Vincent, or in Slough where there are large numbers of Anguillans. One potentially fruitful area for future research would thus seem to be the study of regional variation within Britain.

Another question which has not been considered in the course of the present study is the acquisition of Patois by black children. Frequent reference is made by teachers to the fact that many children who previously showed no evidence of black speech start using Patois in adolescence. This was one of the reasons why we thought it would be most useful to concentrate the present study on adolescent speakers. We have seen that there is considerable variation in the Patois competence of young people, and that this competence is related to their social networks. However, many questions remain unanswered. Is Patois selectively acquired in infancy, lost in childhood and re-acquired in adolescence? We have little knowledge of the Patois competence of black infants and children, and there is plenty of room for longitudinal or cross-sectional studies of language use in these groups.

Finally, the present study has looked at variation in macro-linguistic terms. It has not attempted to consider the complex code-switching behaviour which characterizes much of the speech of many young British blacks, either in terms of its social significance or the linguistic constraints which operate on this behaviour. A detailed description of code-switching is essential for a full understanding of the language use of British Black people. An important start has already been made in this area by Sutcliffe (forthcoming) whose work is based on the West Midlands data used in the present study and Sebba (1984a, b, c, in press) in analyses of London Jamaican.

Further information on the findings in this area will be awaited with considerable interest.

It is regrettable but true that much of research on the language and society of black people in many parts of the world has been informed by, or has helped to perpetuate, negative stereotypes. Hopefully, the main priority of research undertaken in the areas outlined above, or in other directions, will be to present a true and accurate picture of the complexities and depth of black language, rather than further underpinning negative perceptions of the group.

Appendix 1
The linguistic analysis

a) Transcription, coding and analysis

The collection and recording of data have been described in Chapter 6. Some 23 hours of conversation were transcribed orthographically by several different people. Situations containing Patois were allocated to five British Black transcribers; wherever possible, black fieldworkers worked with sessions in which they had actually participated. The other situations were transcribed by English linguists, two of whom came from the West Midlands and were able to "arbitrate" on any points of conflict which arose from unfamiliarity with Black Country Dialect.

Coders then listened to the recordings, marking transcriptions in preparation for analysis with the Oxford Concordance Programme (Hockey & Marriot, 1980). This text analysis programme searches for and provides listings of specified words in their context for given speakers in given situations and thus removes a great deal of the tedium of quantitative analysis. When the variant which is being considered is a word like *dem* or *im*, the text requires no extra preparation. However, phonological variables had to be specially coded for computer recognition. So, too, did certain other variables. There is no way, for instance, in which a computer can distinguish between plural and third person singular present word final -*s*. Although this coding process is also tedious in itself, it has the advantage of greater accuracy over "manual" counts. The way in which it displays the output also offers a wide range of interesting possibilities for further analysis.

Only linguists were used for this coding process. Again white coders were used for English situations, very often working with transcripts provided by other people and so providing a check on the accuracy of transcription. The same black linguist coded all the black situations. All the coded transcripts were double checked by a second linguist.

It is very important to institute a system of cross-checking for a number of reasons. Because a large quantity of speech data was being transcribed and coded by several different individuals, we had to ensure consistency, particularly in the coding. We were also aware of the discrepancies which can arise when native and non-native speakers attempt to analyse the same material, and felt it was essential to draw on black expertise in this area. In actual fact, areas of disagreement were few in number and usually quickly resolved.

b) The Patois index (see Chapter 7)

Some 11 commonly occurring variables formed the basis for the Patois Index. Two of these variables affected pronunciation. Full accounts of Jamaican phonology are contained in Cassidy & Le Page (1967) and Wells (1973, 1982). Wells (1982) describes West Indian English as British rather than American orientated in its phonology but there are nonetheless important differences between the systems. Various differences have also been documented on the level of prosodic features and phonotactic possibilities.

If we compare the sound systems of Received Pronunciation and West Midlands we find that on a phonetic level there are extensive differences but on a phonological level, these differences are few in number. The differences between Jamaican Creole and Received Pronunciation, on the other hand, are important on both phonetic and phonological levels. Table 1 shows the phoneme inventories for all three systems, and the Jamaican and West Midlands reflexes of RP phonemes.

Two phonological variables, one consonant and one vowel, were isolated for analysis. The vowel variable was /ʌ/–/o/. We are dealing with a systemic phonemic difference, rather than different allophones of the same phoneme, and so it is important to specify which variants are to be quantified. Jamaican /o/ is the regular reflex of both West Midlands /ɜ:/ and of West Midlands /ʊ/, and we are interested only in the latter case. A further complication affects lexical subsets in both Jamaican and West Midlands speech. A small number of words containing RP /ʌ/ appear in Jamaican with [a] instead of the [o] which would normally be expected. These words include *one, wonderful,* and *under.* There is also a West Midlands subset which differs from the RP norm. This includes *one, none, nothing* and *mum* which contain [o] rather than the expected [ʊ]. It is thus possible to distinguish between Jamaican /wan/ and West Midlands /won/ and between Jamaican and West Midlands *nothing* in terms of the dental stop versus the

TABLE 1 *Vowel phonemes in Jamaican Creole, RP and West Midlands*

Jamaican Creole	Received Pronunciation (RP)	West Midlands
/ɪ/	/ɪ/	/ɪ/
/ɛ/	/ɛ/	/ɛ/
/a/	/æ/	/æ/
/ʊ/	/ʊ/	/ʊ/
/o/	/ʌ/	
	/ɒ/	/ɒ/
/iː/	/iː/	/iː/
/ie/	/ei/	/ei/
/ai/	/ai/	/ai/
	/ɔi/	
/uː/	/uː/	/uː/
/uo/	/ou/	
/ou/	/au/	/au/
	/ɪə/	/ɪə/
	/ɛə/	
	/ɜː/	/ɜː/
/aa/	/aː/	/aː/
	/ɔː/	/ɔː/
	/ʊa/	/ʊə/

fricative (see below). However, it is necessary to draw on other information, such as the "Englishness" or "Creoleness" of the rest of the clause (see Sutcliffe, forthcoming) in order to decide whether *none* and *mom* are Jamaican or West Midlands variants, and unambiguous decisions are not always possible in such cases. For this reason, it was felt preferable to exclude these words from the analysis.

Consonant variables

The most notable difference between the Jamaican and English consonant systems, in terms of its widespread distribution, is what Wells (1982) calls "TH stopping". The oppositions between [t] and [θ] and [d] and [ð] are neutralized, the alveolar stop being used for both the stop and the fricative phonemes of most British English accents. Thus *tin* and *thin* are pronounced *tin*; both *den* and *then* are pronounced *den*. However, this is a feature which is subject to considerable social and stylistic variation in Jamaica and other parts of the Caribbean. The higher the status of the speaker and the more formal the situation, the greater the proportion of /θ/ variants (cf. Winford, 1972; Young, 1973; Escure, 1979, 1981, 1982, 1983a, b, 1984, in press; for similar observations on this phenomenon in Trinidadian and Belizean settings).

The most important variants of (TH) in the West Midlands would appear to be [f, v]. This pronunciation is usually associated with Cockney speech (cf. Hughes & Trudgill, 1979) and it has also been noted as a feature of London Jamaican (Sebba, 1984a, b, c, in press). When the [f, v] variants were first noted in the speech of the young black people in the sample, the fact that this feature had not been documented in indigenous West Midlands speech led us to believe that we were dealing with a phenomenon which had been diffused to the West Midlands black community via London Jamaican. Cross-checking with examples of speech produced by young white working class people in Dudley, however, showed that this feature appeared variably in most recordings, and that we were dealing with a case of more general northward and westward diffusion of a sound change. Instances of [f, v] where RP would use [θ,ð] were therefore treated as English and not Patois variants.

The other variants of (TH) occur when alveolar articulations precede [θ,ð] in unaccented syllables (cf. Gimson, 1980) giving rise to examples like ['wats zə'taim] and [m nə'mɔ:nin]. Patois has no corresponding phenomenon, preferring peripheral and unreduced vowels as in happin[ɛ]ss, fatt[a] and the definite article [di]. All other variants were therefore treated as English.

Past tense forms

The Patois verb is characteristically uninflected and usually identical in form to the standard English present tense verb stem, though various pre-verbal particles can be used to mark both aspect (see below) and tense. Thus we find examples such as:

Starsky and Hutch spin round in di road
Im tief my pound
John stop up Earl house last night

Pre-verbal particles such as *wen* and *en* (cf. Bailey, 1966) were found at only two points in the present corpus. However, *did*, the past tense marker more usually associated with Barbadian speech, occurred quite often in the speech of a small number of speakers. The occurrences of *did* were nonetheless rare over the sample as a whole, and so the comparison was made only between uninflected Patois and inflected English simple past verb forms. In standard English, verbs divide into two categories: strong verbs which indicate the past tense by an internal vowel change, e.g. *sit/sat*; and weak verbs which add the morpheme (ED), realized as [t, d] or [id] depending on the final consonant of the verb stem, e.g. *walk/walked, jig/jigged, cart/carted*. If we consider the weak verbs, two special cases need more detailed attention. The first concerns a small group of verbs which includes *break, lose* and *leave*, which in Patois take the standard past rather than present form, irrespective of the time reference:

> John can broke di chair wid im hand
> Mary lost di book-dem all di time
> Left me alone!

The second case concerns variation in past tense forms in indigenous British dialects, which is often characterized by generalization of the present tense (cf. Edwards, Trudgill & Weltens, 1984). This is a very widespread phenomenon and in Dudley was found to affect several commonly occurring verbs, including *win* and *come*. In both cases the verbs concerned were omitted from the analysis, as was the standard verb *put* which has the same form in the present and the simple past.

Certain weak verbs also pose difficulties. Those ending in /t/ or /d/ form the past tense by the addition of [ɪd]; the presence of the additional vowel makes it easy to distinguish between present and past tense forms irrespective of the first phoneme of the following word, so that examples of this kind are not problematic. In other cases, however, the addition of the (ED) past tense marker creates a more complex situation. When the following word begins with a consonant the speaker may delete t/d in order to simplify the resultant consonant cluster. A great deal of attention has been paid in the literature to the question of t/d deletion (cf. Labov, 1972; Guy, 1980), since, in groups whose speech is characterized by a rather reduced range of consonant clusters (such as speakers of Black English Vernacular), there are obvious implications for whether there is an underlying past tense form. However, even those speakers who use a wider range of consonant clusters are likely to delete t/d in certain environments in connected speech. For this reason, only weak past tense forms in [ɪd] and those occurring before /h, w, j, r/ (cf. Gimson, 1980) and vowels were included in the analysis.

Initial analysis treated strong and weak verbs separately. This practice was later abandoned partly because of the low incidence of strong verbs, but mainly because there was no evidence of separate patterning for the two classes of verbs.

Third person singular present -s

Another consequence of the invariant verb form is that there is no subject-verb concord in present tense reference.

> Duppy know who im fraid *(The ghost knows who he frightens)*
> Who pop style in here?
> David use dat often

Occasionally this gives rise to alternative interpretations, and there is difficulty in distinguishing between past and present reference:

John go a yaad in di afternoon — *John went/goes home in the*
                                                                        afternoon
Winston run fast — *Winston runs/ran fast*

However, examples where context cues did not immediately clarify the speaker's intention were very rare, and the problem was circumvented by excluding such examples from the analysis.

Plurals

The Patois noun, like the Patois verb, is characteristically invariant, and plural reference is usually clarified contextually:

Where you go most time?
He give me two book

Count nouns may also take the definite plural marker (di) . . . dem:

Di whole of dem hate di black-dem inna di school — *all of them*
                                                                        hate the blacks in the school.
Clovis gone up a Elaine fi you record-dem — *Clovis went up*
                                                                        Elaine's for your records

So, too, may proper nouns, in which case the most appropriate gloss would seem to be "and friends" (Beverley-dem naa like dat — *Beverley and her friends don't like that*) but, in order to ensure that we were comparing like with like, these "associative" plurals were not included in the analysis. Also excluded were Patois count nouns like *shoes* and *peas* which have the same form as the standard plural, irrespective of whether the speaker is making singular or plural reference.

Le Page (1972) draws attention to a possible area of difficulty in the quantification of plural nouns. Because the Patois verb is invariant, subject-verb concord cannot be used to help in deciding whether a noun is singular or plural. Drawing on the example:

/taiga kyaan klaim trii/

he identifies two possible interpretations:

tigers can't climb trees
Tiger (personification) can't climb trees

He points to the French example "le tigre ne peut pas monter dans un arbre" which is functionally the same as the Jamaican example in that it can also be translated in two ways, and warns against the dangers of imposing an alien semantic distinction on Patois by deciding, on the basis of an English framework, that the speaker may be making plural reference. While acknowledging the validity of this observation, it should be noted that very few comparable examples occurred in the present corpus and context almost invariably disambiguated cases of singular and plural reference. However, where there was any element of doubt, the example was excluded from the analysis.

Pronouns

In Broad Jamaican Patois, pronouns are unmarked for either sex or case:

me — I, me, my	we — we, us, our
yu — you, your	unu — you, your
im— he, him, his, she, her	dem — they, them, their
i — it, its	

There is, however, an alternative possibility for marking possession, namely the addition of *fi* to the pronoun:

mi hear fi-me Daddy say it — *I heard my Daddy say it*
you have to learn it cos you live inna fi-dem land — *you have to
learn it because you live in their land*

This *fi*-marking of possession was restricted to very few tokens in only a small proportion of speakers, and it was therefore felt to be more appropriate to consider this feature in the discussion of Patois competence below than in the construction of a Patois index of frequently occurring variables.

Certain of these Patois pronoun forms contrast very clearly with their English translations and are therefore very suitable for inclusion in a quantitative study. Thus *me* as subject pronoun is easily distinguished from standard and West Midlands *I*. However, the object pronoun has the same form in both Patois and English, and the possessive pronoun also occurs variably as /me/ in the West Midlands. The second person singular, too, is unsuitable for inclusion in the analysis. The Patois and English forms in subject and object positions are so similar that it would be extremely difficult to distinguish between them with any degree of confidence when working with rapid, connected, tape-recorded speech. In contrast, *im* is easily identified as subject and possessive pronoun, and as object pronoun in female but not male reference. When dealing with the third person singular we need also to note that the Black Country feminine subject form used variably in Dudley is *her*:

Her cooks our Angela something different
Her likes to do that

Similarly when dealing with plural references, *we* can be contrasted with the English object and possessive but not the subject pronouns; *unu* is easily distinguished from all cases of the second person plural; and *dem* can be contrasted with the English subject and possessive pronouns.

me, *im* and *dem* all occurred often and relative frequencies of English and Patois variants could therefore be calculated without difficulty. However, other Patois pronouns, notably *we* (object and possessive), *unu* and possessive pronouns with *fi-* appeared so infrequently that it was unrealistic to consider each separately. They were therefore conflated in a separate group and considered in the discussion of Patois competence below.

DO+neg

In the absence of an operator such as *could* or *had* in standard English (see Quirk & Greenbaum, 1976: 2.3), the auxiliary DO+ neg, followed by the bare infinitive, is used to negate positive sentences.

She goes back home tomorrow — *She doesn't go back home*
$\qquad\qquad\qquad\qquad\qquad\qquad\qquad\qquad$ *tomorrow*
He saw her do it — *He didn't see her do it*

In the West Midlands we find the variable use of *doe* for *doesn't* and *day* for *didn't*:

John doe like her — *John doesn't like her*
They day do it — *They didn't do it*

The Patois system of negation is very different. Bailey (1966) suggests that *no* is a universal negator. (Bailey's transcriptions are phonemic, and contrast with the orthographic conventions adopted elsewhere in this book.)

Dem no have di answer — *they haven't got the answer*
Dat no matter — *that doesn't matter*

With the progressive, *no+a* are merged and we find *naa:*

mi naa tell im dat — *I'm not telling him that*
Im naa guo a yaad — *he isn't going home*

Bailey also suggests *neba* as a negator when all or part of the action is set in the past:

mi neba nuo se Jan gaan — *I didn't know John had left*

and the use of *duon* in sentences where the main verb is a psychic state verb, or one which indicates habitual action:

> im duon wier shuuz nontaal — *he doesn't wear shoes at all*

It is difficult to evaluate Bailey's claim for *duon*, since she cites only the above example. Certainly, in the present corpus, the use of *duon* in clauses otherwise marked as Patois was rare, and there was a strong preference for *no* or *naa*. This observation applies to both psychic state verbs and verbs which indicate habitual activity.

> Me no care if anybody see dis
> Me no know what fi put
> You no buy reggae and soul?
> Me no talk English

It is possible that the preference for *no* and *naa* is an overgeneralization in the British trend towards basilectal forms. However, the British pattern would appear to be mirrored in a Belizean context where Escure (1979) reports that Do+neg sentences are characteristic of acrolectal speech, and makes no reference to the limited use of *duon* in the basilect. This would lead to the suggestion that *duon* is an acrolectal innovation in Jamaica, though in the absence of sociolinguistic studies it is clearly not possible to be sure.

Infinitives

English infinitives can be preceded by "to"; infinitives in basilectal Caribbean varieties can be preceded by "fi" (as in Jamaican Patois) or "fu" (as in Guyanese and Vincentian).

> You ask im how fi cook rice im no know
> Mi no know where fi put dis one
> Dem want me fi go up dere go tell dem
> You hafi (have fi) underline dem you know

Copulas

The copula-auxiliary complex is represented uniformly in English with the verb "to be". The realization of this verb is subject to a great deal of dialect variation. (Edwards *et al.*, 1984) and the following forms are found to alternate with the standard in West Midlands speech:

Copula-auxiliary complex in West Midlands speech

Present tense affirmative

I (a)m	We (a)m
You (a)m	You (a)m
He, She, It (i)s	They (a)m

Present tense negative
All persons: *ay*, e.g. We ay coming, He ay lying

Past tense affirmative

I was	We was
You was	You was
He, She, It was	They was

Past tense negative
All persons: *wor*, e.g. He wor saying that; I wor running

Jamaican and other Caribbean varieties treat this area of syntax in a very distinct way. A three way distinction occurs between those sentences with nominal predicates, those with locatives and those with adjectives. Thus, in Jamaican Patois there is an equating verb *a* which connects two nominals, or a nominal with a possessive *fi* — phrase:

Di first one a me woman — *the first one is my woman*
It a fi-me — *It's mine*

There is a locating verb *deh* which is followed by a locative complement or modifier:

Kunta Kinte deh pan di B-side — *Kunta Kinte is on the B-side*
When me deh at school, di whole a dem hate me — *When I was at school, they all hated me*

The treatment of adjectives is also quite distinct. Sentences such as:

John ready
Mary good

have tended to be described in the literature as examples of zero copula. There is, however, abundant evidence of the verb-like behaviour of these "adjectives". They occur, for example, with the present continuative marker *a* and the past marker *did* (see below):

John a ready — *John is getting ready*
Mary did good — *Mary was being good*

This suggests that adjectives might more properly be analysed as forming a subcategory of stative verbs.

The equating verb *a*, like the locating verb, occurs in the speech of only a small number of speakers and then only rarely. These two features were not therefore included in the construction of the Patois index. However, their presence was carefully noted in terms of the analysis of Patois com-

petence below. For present purposes, English instances of adjectives with
either the standard or the Black Country variants of the verb "to be" were
expressed as a proportion of Patois instances of adjectives behaving as
stative verbs and verbs which co-occurred with the continuative marker *a* or
its negative equivalent *naa*.

c) The Patois competence scale (see Chapter 8)

The Patois competence scale draws heavily on the Patois index. It also
includes a number of features which occurred too infrequently to be incor-
porated into the Patois index. It was explained in the discussion of pronouns
above, for instance, that while the Patois variants of I, she/he/his/her, and
they/their all occurred sufficiently often to be considered separately in the
Patois index, other Patois pronoun variants — object and possessive *we, unu*
and *fi* possessives — occurred far less frequently and in the speech of a
relatively small proportion of speakers. They were thus considered col-
lectively in the discussion of competence, rather than as part of the Patois
index. Similarly the equating verb *a* and the locating verb *deh* and the past
marker *did* (see Copulas, above) occurred in only in a small proportion of
speakers and were therefore best treated under the heading of competence.

The construction of a competence scale also allowed for finer differentiation than had been possible in the consideration of the Patois index.
Patois adjectival verbs and continuatives both of which required copulas in
English, occurred fairly infrequently in the data, and so were conflated in
the construction of the index. For the present purposes, however, they were
considered separately. *Did*, the past tense marker, was found in the speech
of only a small number of speakers and was therefore included in the Patois
competence scale but not the index. Finally, although both uninflected
Patois plurals and plurals in *-dem* were compared with inflected English
nouns, it was noticed that only a small proportion of speakers used *-dem*,
and so the two Patois variants were considered separately.

Three other features not previously discussed were considered in the
calculation of competence scores — interrogation, focus and psychic state
transitive verbs.

Questions

Questions in English can be marked either by intonation, by changes in
word order alone, by the introduction of question words which are followed
either by declarative sentence order or the use of DO as an operator, or by
the use of DO as operator and changes in word order:

He walked home?
Can he walk home?
Who walked home?
Who did you see?
Did he walk home?

In Patois questions are marked either by changes in intonation or by question words which are preposed to the declarative form of the sentence:

Di man see im sister?
Who di man see?

Any comparison of Patois and English questions had to be made between Patois questions, with or without a question word, which would have required the use of DO in English, or questions with question words which would have required inversion:

You no see?
Where di gospel deh?
So what dat mean?

Focus

Methods of marking focus differ considerably from one language to another. In Patois, the focussed element is moved to sentence initial position and adjoined by *a* (Bailey, 1966; Bickerton, 1981):

a Mieri hit di bwai
a di bwai Mieri hit
a hit Mieri hit di bwai

In English focus can be marked in a number of ways (Quirk & Greenbaum, 1976). All elements can be focussed using stress and intonation:

Mary hit the boy
Mary hit the *boy*
Mary *hit* the boy

Subjects and objects can also be given thematic prominence by the use of cleft sentences which divides a single clause into two separate sections, each with its own verb:

It was Mary who hit the boy
It was the boy Mary hit

Alternatively, all elements, including the verb, can be focussed using a pseudo-cleft sentence:

The boy was who Mary hit
Mary was who hit the boy
What Mary did was hit the boy

The use of *a* as a focussing particle was fairly common in the data. However, it was decided to exclude this feature from the Patois index because of the wide range of corresponding English constructions and the problems which this would have created for any discussion of equivalence (cf. Dines, 1980).

Psychic state transitive verbs

In Patois we find that verbs like feel, hear, mean, know and believe, which refer to the psychic state of the subject nominal and have either a nominal or a sentence as object, can be followed by *seh* (cf. Bailey, 1966):

> You feel seh you can chat Patois like me? — *You feel you can talk*
> *Patois like me?*
>
> Tell him seh you naa pay — *Tell me you're not paying*
>
> Dat mean seh you woulda see him now — *That means you'd see*
> *him now*

The most probable explanation for this form lies in the influence of certain West African languages (cf. Cassidy, 1961; Sebba, 1984a) in which "say" follows a previous verb of telling or commanding and acts as a complementizer. (In Akan, concidentally, "say" is translated as *se*). Sebba (1984a) reports that this is a feature of the "English" variety of young London black people. The same does not appear to hold for the West Midlands where *seh* was found only once in the English situations in our corpus. It was, however, a regular feature in the speech of about a third of the participants in Patois situations.

Appendix 2
Statistical methods

Standard statistical techniques were used to do the analyses. The task was to determine the extent to which a number of response variables (Patois frequency scores in Chapter 7; Patois competence scores in Chapter 8; and Patois pattern scores in Chapter 9) were related to a series of explanatory variables (sex, education, network, acquiescence–criticalness of the subject). Linear regression methods, generalized to cope with quantitative variables such as sex, were used (see, for example, Draper & Smith, 1981). All the statistical calculations were carried out using GLIM (Baker & Nelder, 1978), a computer package suitable for analysing data with this type of structure.

As usual the effect of the explanatory variables was assessed by the size of the reduction in the residual sum of squares when that variable was included in the model. The non-orthogonality of the explanatory variables meant that terms had to be added in various orders — a tedious process, but one which seldom left any doubt as to which were the important effects. A consequence of this is that a standard analysis of variance table cannot be presented unambiguously. Tables (a), (b), (c) and (d) below give sums of squares for each of the effects when that term was the last added to the model. Residuals (observed value minus value predicted by the model) were studied to ensure that the assumptions of the analysis were reasonable and that no systematic effects had been missed. In all cases probability plots of the residuals showed that inferences are not likely to be incorrect due to the non-normality of the data.

149

a) Patois frequency (Chapter 7)

The Effects of Background Variables on Patois Frequency

	ss	*df*	*F-value*	*Significance*
Acqu.–Crit.	998	1	10.955	1%
Sex. Education	881	1	9.671	1%
Network	666	1	7.311	1%
Education×Acqu.–Crit.	353	1	3.875	n.s.
Education×Network	315	1	3.458	n.s.
Sex×Network	57	1	0.626	n.s.
Sex×Acqu.–Crit.	248	1	2.722	n.s.
Residual	3370	37	$s^2=91.1$	

b) Patois competence (Chapter 8)

The Effects of Background Variables on Patois Competence

	ss	*df*	*F-value*	*Significance*
Word count	65.8	1	9.676	1%
Network	381.8	1	56.147	0.1%
Sex	8.8	1	1.294	n.s.
Education	13.9	1	2.029	n.s.
Acqu.–Crit.	1.7	1	0.250	n.s.
Residual	265.2	39	$s^2=6.8$	

c) Patois patterns (Chapter 9)

The Effects of Background Variables on Patois Patterns

	ss	*df*	*F-value*	*Significance*
Network	15.61	1	15.2	0.1%
Education	0.86	1	0.8	n.s.
Residual	42.10	41	$s^2=1.027$	

d) Interview sequence (Chapter 6)

The effect of recording sequence on language use was assessed by comparing the Patois frequency of those speakers who were interviewed by the white researcher first and last. Angular transformations were used on the data. The interaction of sex and education, network and acquiescence–criticalness had already been identified as important factors for these scores, and were removed first.

	ss	*df*	*F-value*	*Significance*
Sequence	0.0164	1	1.12	n.s.
Residual	0.5352	37	$s^2=0.0146$	

Appendix 3
The questionnaire

1. How would you describe your time in school?
   very happy/quite happy/OK/quite unhappy/very unhappy
2. How many teachers do you think were prejudiced against black children?
   all or almost all/more than half/about half/less than half/none or very few
3. What about white people as a whole?
   all or almost all/more than half/about half/less than half/none or very few
4. How do you think teachers found *you* as a person?
   very co-operative/quite co-operative/OK/quite difficult/very difficult
5. How do you think teachers found the way you worked?
   very hardworking/quite hardworking/OK/quite lazy/very lazy
6. Think of your three closest friends. Are they black or white:
   friend 1: black/white
   friend 2: black/white
   friend 3: black/white
7. Ring any of the following places where you and these friends go together:
   friend 1: youth club   church   sport   shcool/work
   friend 2: youth club   church   sport   school/work
   friend 3: youth club   church   sport   school/work
8. Ring any of the following kinds of music that you like:
   classical   folk   Gospel   soul   rock   jazz   funk   jazz funk
   steel band   calypso   reggae   dub   lovers rock   other (please say which)
9. What kind of music do you actually buy?
10. Do you see white friends from school or work socially?
    often/sometimes/never

151

11. Do you and your white neighbours visit each other's houses?
    often/sometimes/never
12. What do you think of the way the police treat black people?
    very fair/quite fair/OK/quite unfair/very unfair
13. If you were stopped and questioned by the police and you had done
    nothing wrong, what do you think would be the best thing to do?
    try to get away/co-operate but complain/co-operate without complaint
14. How important are the African roots of your culture to you?
    very important/quite important/important/not very important
    not all important
15. Do you think "Jamaica talk" such as *me a pop style, ennit?* is:
    broken English/a dialect/a language
16. Do *you* "pop style"?
    often/sometimes/never
17. Who would use proverbs such as *Fire deh a mus-mus tail im tink a cool
    breeze?*
    only grandparents/only parents/some parents and some children
18. Do *you* know any proverbs? If so, could you write one down?
19. A recent report said that only between 10 and 20% of British born black
    people can speak "Jamaica talk" or "Patwa". What do you think this
    figure should be?
    all or nearly all/more than half/half/less than half/none or very few
20. Do *you* talk "Patwa"?
    often/sometimes/never

Bibliography

ABRAHAMS, R. 1972a, The training of the man of words in talking sweet. *Language in Society*, 1(1): 15–30.
— 1972b, Joking: the training of the man of words in talking broad. In T. KOCHMAN (ed.), *Rappin' and Stylin' Out*. Chicago: University of Illinois Press.
AKERS, G. 1981, *Phonological variation in the Jamaican continuum*. Ann Arbor: Karoma Press.
ALLEN, S. 1982, Confusing categories and neglecting contradictions. In E. CASHMORE & B. TROYNA (eds), *Black Youth in Crisis*. London: Allen and Unwin. pp. 143–58.
ALLEYNE, M. 1971, The Cultural Matrix of Creolization. In D. HYMES (ed.), *Pidginization and Creolization*. Cambridge: Cambridge University Press. pp. 169–86.
— 1980, *Comparative Afro-American*. Ann Arbor, Michigan: Karoma Press.
ANDERSON, E. 1979, The reading behaviour of a group of children of families of West Indian origin. M.Phil thesis, University of Nottingham.
ASSOCIATION OF TEACHERS OF ENGLISH TO PUPILS FROM OVERSEAS (ATEPO) (Birmingham Branch) 1970, *Work Group on West Indian Pupils Report*.
BAGLEY, C., BART, M. & WONG, J. 1979, Antecedents of scholastic success in West Indian ten year olds in London. In G. VERMA & C. BAGLEY (eds), *Race, Education and Identity*. London: Macmillan. pp. 84–94.
BAILEY, B. 1966, *Jamaican Creole Syntax*. Cambridge: Cambridge University Press.
— 1971, Can dialect boundaries be defined? In D. HYMES (ed.), *Pidginization and Creolization*. Cambridge: Cambridge University Press, pp. 341–48.
BAKER, G. 1976, Creole language features in the speech of West Indian Primary School Children in Nottingham. M.Phil thesis, University of Nottingham.
BAKER, R. & NELDER, J. 1978, *The GLIM Manual*. Oxford: Numerical Algorithms Group.
BARATZ, J. 1968, Reply to Dr. Raph's article on speech and language deficits in culturally deprived children. *Journal of Speech and Hearing Disorders*, 33: 299–300.
BARATZ, J. & SHUY, R. (eds) 1969, *Teaching Black Children to Read*. Washington DC: Center for Applied Linguistics.
BART, W. & KRUS, D. 1973, An ordering-theoretic method to determine hierarchies among items. *Educational and Psychological Measurement*, 33: 291–300.

153

BEREITER, C. & ENGELMANN, S. 1966, *Teaching Disadvantaged Children in the Pre-School*. Englewood Cliffs, New Jersey: Prentice-Hall.

BICKERTON, D. 1973, On the nature of a creole continuum, *Language*, 49: 640–49.

— 1975, *The Dynamics of a Creole system*. Cambridge: Cambridge University Press.

— 1981, *Roots of Language*. Ann Arbor: Karoma Press.

BLACK PEOPLES' PROGRESSIVE ASSOCIATION AND REDBRIDGE COMMUNITY RELATIONS COUNCIL 1978, *Cause for Concern*.

BLANK, M. 1970, Some philosophical influences underlying preschool intervention for disadvantaged children. In F. WILLIAMS (ed.), *Language and Poverty*. Chicago: Markham. pp. 62–80.

BLOM, J. & GUMPERZ, J. 1972, Social meanings in linguistic structures: code switching in Norway. In J. GUMPERZ & D. HYMES (eds), *Directions in Sociolinguistics*. New York: Holt, Rinehart and Winston. pp. 407–34.

BORTONI DE FIGUEIREDO RICARDO, S. M. 1983, Urbanisation of rural dialects in Brazil. Ph.D thesis, University of Lancaster.

BOURHIS, R. & GILES, H. 1976, The language of cooperation in Wales: a field study. *Language Sciences*, 42: 13–16.

— 1977, The language of intergroup distinctiveness. In H. GILES (ed.), *Language, Ethnicity and Intergroup Relations*. London: Academic Press. pp. 119–36.

BOURHIS, R., GILES, H., LEYENS, J. P. & TAJFEL, H. 1979, Psycholinguistic distinctiveness: language divergence in Belgium. In H. GILES & R. SAINT CLAIR (eds), *Language and Social Psychology*. Oxford: Basil Blackwell and Baltimore: University Park Press. pp. 158–85.

BREINBURG, P. 1983, Linguistic shift — urban creoles and the black child in European inner city schools. Paper given at the York Conference on Urban Creoles.

— in press, Perception and response to language — the Afro-Caribbean case. In D. SUTCLIFFE & A. WONG (eds), *Language and the British Black Experience*. Oxford: Blackwell.

BRESNAN, J. & KAPLAN, R. 1982, Grammars as mental representations of language. In J. BRESNAN (ed.), *The Mental Representation of Grammatical Relations*. Cambridge, Mass: MIT Press.

BROWN, C. 1984, *Black and White Britain*. London: Policy Studies Institute.

BULLOCK, SIR A. 1975, *A Language for Life*. London: HMSO.

CARBY, H. 1980, Multicultural Fictions. Occasional Stencilled Paper No. 58, Centre for Contemporary Cultural Studies/University of Birmingham.

CARRINGTON, L. & BORELY, D. (eds) 1977, *The Language Arts Syllabus, 1975: Comment and Countercomment*. University of Saint Augustine, Trinidad.

CARTER, H. 1982, The tonal system of Jamaican English. Paper given at the Fourth Biennial Conference of the Society for Caribbean Linguistics, Paramaribo, Suriname.

CASHMORE, E. 1979, *Rastaman: the Rastafarian Movement in England*. London: Allen & Unwin.

CASHMORE, E. & TROYNA, B. (eds) 1982, *Black Youth in Crisis*. London: Allen and Unwin.

CASSIDY, F. 1961, *Jamaica Talk*. Cambridge: Cambridge University Press.

CASSIDY, F. & LE PAGE, R. 1967, *Dictionary of Jamaican English*. Cambridge: Cambridge University Press.

CENTRE FOR CONTEMPORARY CULTURAL STUDIES 1982, *The Empire Strikes Back: Race and Racism in 70s Britain*. London: Hutchinson.

CHAMBERS, J. & TRUDGILL, P. 1980, *Dialectology*. Cambridge: Cambridge University Press.

CHESHIRE, J. 1982, *Variation in an English Dialect: a Sociolinguistic Analysis*. Cambridge: Cambridge University Press.

CHIN, W. & SIMSOVA, S. 1981, *Information sheets on Chinese readers*. Research Report No. 7, School of Librarianship, Polytechnic of North London.

CHOMSKY, N. 1965, *Aspects of the Theory of Syntax*, Cambridge, Mass: MIT Press.

CHOMSKY, N. & HALLE, M. 1968, *The Sound Patterns of English*. New York: Harper and Row.

COARD, B. 1971, *How the West Indian Child is Made Educationally Sub-Normal in the British School System*. London: New Beacon Books.

CONOLLY, Y., CAMERON, G. & SINGHAM, S. 1981, *Mango Spice*. London: A. & C. Black.

COVENEY, A. 1985, Sociolinguistic variables in grammar (or why should the sociolinguistic variable stop?). Manuscript, Department of French Studies, University of Newcastle.

CRAIG, D. 1976, Bidialectal education: Creole and Standard in the West Indies. *International Journal of the Sociology of Language*, 8: 93–134.

— 1981, Review of V. K. Edwards 'The West Indian Language Issue in British Schools'. *Language in Society*, 10: 398–400.

CRUMP, S. 1979, The Language of West Indian children and its relevance for schools. Unpublished MA dissertation, University of London Institute of Education. Not available for loan.

CUMMINS, J. 1984, *Bilingualism and Special Education: Issues in Assessment and Pedagogy*. Clevedon, Avon: Multilingual Matters.

DALPHINES, M. 1982, Approaches to the study of Creole languages — the case for West Africa languages. In *French Creole*, Occasional Papers on Caribbean languages and dialects, No. 2. London: Caribbean Communications Project, Arawidi Ltd., UK.

— in press, *Caribbean and African Languages: Social History, Language, Literature and Education*. London: Karia Press.

D'COSTA, J. 1981, Review of The West Indian Language Issue in British Schools by V. K. Edwards. *Harvard Educational Review*: 193–97.

DANIEL, W. 1968, *Racial Discrimination in England*. Harmondsworth: Penguin.

DE CAMP, D. 1971, Towards a Generative Analysis of a Post-Creole Continuum. In D. HYMES (ed.), *Pidginization and Creolization*. Cambridge: Cambridge University Press. pp. 349–70.

DE LANGE, D. & KOSMIN, B. 1979, *Community Resources for a Community Survey*. Research of the Board of Deputies of British Jews. London.

DEPARTMENT OF EDUCATION AND SCIENCE 1970, *Statistics of Education*. London: HMSO.

DINES, E. 1980, Variation in discourse — "and stuff like that". *Language in Society*, 9: 13–33.

DORIAN, N. 1981, *Language Death: the life cycle of a Scottish Gaelic Dialect*. Philadelphia: University of Pennsylvania Press.

— 1982, Defining the speech community to include its working margins. In S. ROMAINE (ed.), *Sociolinguistic Variation in Speech Communities*. London: Edward Arnold. pp. 25–34.

DOUGLAS-COWIE, E. 1978, Linguistic codeswitching in a Northern Irish village: social interaction and social ambition. In P. TRUDGILL (ed.), *Sociolinguistic Patterns in British English*. London: Edward Arnold. pp. 37–51.

DRAPER, N. & SMITH, H. 1981, *Applied Regression Analysis*. 2nd edition. New York: Wiley.

DRIVER, G. 1980, How West Indians do better at school (especially the girls). *New Society*, 17 January: 111–14.

DULAY, H., BURT, M. & KRASHEN, S. 1982, *Language Two*. New York: Oxford University Press.

EDWARDS, J. 1979, *Language and Disadvantage*. London: Edward Arnold.

EDWARDS, V. 1976, Effects of dialect on the comprehension of West Indian Children. *Educational Research*, 18(2): 83–95.

— 1978a, Language Attitudes and Underperformance in West Indian Children. *Educational Review*, 30(1): 51–58.

— 1978b, Dialect interference in West Indian children. *Language and Speech*, 21(1).

— 1979, *The West Indian Language Issue in British Schools: Challenges and Responses*. London: Routledge and Kegan Paul.

— 1980, British Black English: a bibliographical essay on the language of children of West Indian origin. *Sage Race Relations Abstracts*, 5(3 & 4): 1–25.

— 1983, *Language in Multicultural Classrooms*. London: Batsford.

— 1984, *Language Policy in Multicultural Britain*. In J. EDWARDS (ed.), *Linguistic Minorities, Policies and Pluralism*. London: Academic Press. pp. 49–80.

EDWARDS, V., TRUDGILL, P. & WELTENS, B. 1984, *The Grammar of English Dialect*. London: Economic and Social Research Council.

EDWARDS, W. 1975, Sociolinguistic behaviour in rural and urban circumstances in Guyana. D.Phil thesis, University of York.

— 1984, Socializing the continuum: Guyanese Sociolinguistic Culture as Social networks. Paper presented to the 5th Biennial Conference of the Society for Caribbean Linguistics, Mona, Jamaica.

ELDER, J. D. 1973, *Song Games from Trinidad and Tobago*. 2nd edition. Port of Spain, Trinidad: National Cultural Council Publications.

ESCURE, G. 1979, Linguistic Variation and ethnic interaction in Belize: Creole/Carib. In H. GILES & B. SAINT-JACQUES (eds), *Language and Ethnic Relations*. Oxford: Pergamon. pp. 101–15.

— 1981, Decreolization in a creole continuum: Belize. In A. HIGHFIELD & A. VALDMAN (eds), *Historicity and Variation in Creole Studies*. Ann Arbor: Karoma Press. pp. 27–39.

— 1982, Contrastive patterns of intragroup and intergroup interaction in the creole continuum of Belize. *Language in Society*, 11: 239–64.

— 1983a, The use of Creole as interlanguage by the Black Carib of Belize. In F. INGEMANN (ed.), *Mid-America Linguistics Conference Papers*. University of Kansas, Lawrence, Kansas. pp. 271–82.

— 1983b, Sexual differentiation and copula variability in a creole continuum. In G. GILBERT (ed.), *Pidgin and Creole Languages: essays in memory of John Reinecke*. Ann Arbor: Karoma Press.

— 1984, The Belizean copula: a case of semantactic shift. In L. CARRINGTON (ed.), *Studies in Caribbean Language*.

— in press, The Acquisition of Creole by Urban and Rural Black Caribs in Belize. In M. SEBBA & L. TODD (eds), *York Papers in Linguistics, 11*.

FIGUEROA, P. 1982, The West Indian experience in *The Open University*. pp. 29–53.

FILLMORE, C., KEMPLER, D. & WANG, W. (eds), 1979, *Individual differences in language ability and language behaviour*. New York: Academic Press.

FULLER, M. 1980, Black girls in a London comprehensive school. In R. DEEM (ed.), *Schooling for Women's Work*. London: Routledge and Kegan Paul. pp. 52–65.
— 1983, Qualified criticism, critical qualifications. In L. BARTON & S. WALKER (eds), *Race, Class and Education*. Beckenham: Croom Helm. pp. 166–90.

GAL, S. 1979, *Language Shift: Social Determinants of Linguistic Change in Bilingual Austria*. New York: Academic Press.

GARRISON, L. 1979, *Black Youth, Rastafarianism and the Identity Crisis in Britain*. London: ACER Project.

GIBSON, K. 1982, Tense and aspect in Guyanese Creole: a syntactic, semantic and pragmatic analysis. D.Phil thesis, University of York.

GILES, H. 1971, Patterns of evaluation to RP, South Welsh and Somerset accented speech. *British Journal of Social and Clinical Psychology*, 10: 280–81.
— 1973, Accent mobility: a model and some data. *Anthropological Linguistics*, 15: 87–105.
— (ed.) 1977a, *Language, Ethnicity and Intergroup Relations*. London: Academic Press.
— 1977b, Linguistic differentiation in ethnic groups. In H. TAJFEL (ed.), *Differentiation Between Social Groups: Studies in the Social Psychology of Intergroup Relations*. London: Academic Press. pp. 361–86.

GILES, H., BOURHIS, R. & TAYLOR, D. 1977, Towards a theory of language in ethnic group relations. In H. GILES (ed.), *Language, Ethnicity and Intergroup Relations*. London: Academic Press. pp. 307–48.

GILES, H. & POWESLAND, P. 1975, *Speech Style and Social Evaluation*. London: Academic Press.

GILES, H., TAYLOR, D. & BOURHIS, R. 1973, Towards a theory of interpersonal accommodation through language: some Canadian data. *Language in Society*, 2, 177–92.

GIMSON, A. 1980, *An Introduction to the Pronunciation of English*. 3rd edition. London: Edward Arnold.

GOLLASCH, F. 1982, *Language and Literacy: the Selected Writings of K. S. Goodman*. Vol. 1: *Process, Theory, Research*. London: Routledge and Kegan Paul.

GOODMAN, K. & BUCK, C. 1973, Dialect barriers to reading comprehension revisited. *The Reading Teacher*, 27(1): 6–12.

GOODY, J. 1981, *Language and Dialect in the Multi-Ethnic Classroom*. Inner London Education Authority.

GORDON, J. 1981, *Verbal Deficit: a Critique*. London: Croom Helm.

GUY, G. 1980, Variation in the group and the individual: the case of final stop deletion. In W. LABOV (ed.), *Locating Language in Time and Space*. New York: Academic Press. pp. 1–35.

HADI, S. 1976, Some Language Issues. Unpublished paper based for a survey undertaken as part of the Schools Council/NFER 'Education for a Multiracial Society' project.

HANNERZ, U. 1974, Black ghetto culture and community. In C. BELL & H. NEWBY (eds), *Readings in Sociology of Community*. London: Cassell. pp. 149–74.

HARRIS, J. 1984, Syntactic variation and dialect divergence. *Journal of Linguistics*, 20: 303–27.

HAWKINS, E. 1984, *Awareness of Language*. Cambridge: Cambridge University Press.

HEBDIGE, D. 1976, Reggae, rudies and rastas. In S. HALL & T. JEFFERSON (eds), *Resistance Through Ritual: Youth Sub-Cultures in Post-War Britain.* London: Hutchinson. pp. 135–54.

HENRY, I., JOSHUA, H. & SARGEANT, R. 1982, Power, Culture and Identity: the case of the Afro-Caribbean people, in *The Open University.* pp. 54–66.

HMSO 1973, *Select Committee on Race Relations and Immigration, Session 1972–3, Education,* Volume 1: *Report.* London: HMSO.

HERNANDEZ-CHAVEZ, E., COHEN, A. & BELTRAMO, A. 1975, *El Lenguaje de los Chicanos.* Arlington, Virginia: Center for Applied Linguistics.

HERSKOVITS, M. 1937, *Suriname Folklore.* London: Oxford University Press.

HESS, R. & SHIPMAN, V. 1965, Early experience and the socialization of cognitive modes in children. *Child Development,* 36: 869–86.

HEWITT, R. 1982, White adolescent Creole users and the politics of friendship. *Journal of Multilingual and Multicultural Development,* 3: 217–32.

HIRO, D. 1973, *Black British, White British.* Harmondsworth: Penguin.

HOCKEY, S. & MARRIOT, I. 1980, *Oxford Concordance Programme Users' Manual.* Oxford: Oxford University Computing Service.

HOUSTON, S. 1973, A re-examination of some assumptions about the language of the disadvantaged child. In M. MOSS (ed.), *Deprivation and Disadvantage?* Milton Keynes: The Open University Press. pp. 64–70.

HUDSON, R. 1980, *Sociolinguistics.* Cambridge: Cambridge University Press.

HUGHES, A. & TRUDGILL, P. 1979, *English Accents and Dialects. An Introduction to Social and Regional Varieties of British English.* London: Edward Arnold.

HYMES, D. (ed.) 1971, *Pidginization and Creolization.* Cambridge: Cambridge University Press.

— 1979, Sapir, Competence and Voices. In C. FILLMORE, D. KEMPLER & W. WANG (eds), *Individual Differences in Language Ability and Language Behaviour.* New York: Academic Press. pp. 33–46.

JAHANGIRI, N. & HUDSON, R. 1982, Patterns of variation in Tehrani Persian. In S. ROMAINE (ed.), *Sociolinguistic Variation in Speech Communities.* London: Edward Arnold. pp. 49–64.

JENKINS, R. & TROYNA, B. 1983, Educational Myths, Labour Market Realities. In B. TROYNA & D. SMITH (eds), *Racism, School and the Labour market.* Leicester: National Youth Bureau. pp. 5–16.

JOHNSON, J. 1978, Ballad for You. *Race Today,* January/February.

JOHNSON, L. 1976, The Reggae Rebellion. *New Society,* 36, No. 714: 589.

— 1981, *Inglan is a Bitch.* Race Today Publications.

JOOS, M. 1966, *Readings in Linguistics 1.* Chicago and London: Chicago University Press.

KACHRU, B. 1978, Toward structuring code-mixing: an Indian perspective. *International Journal of the Sociology of Language,* 16: 27–46.

KATZ, J. 1981, *Language and Other Abstract Objects.* Oxford: Basil Blackwell.

KENRICK, D. 1982, We speak broken French at home. In *French Creole.* Occasional Papers on Caribbean language and dialects, No. 2. London: Caribbean Communication Project, Arawidi Ltd., UK.

KING, R. 1969, *Historical Linguistics and Generative Grammar.* Englewood Cliffs, New Jersey: Prentice-Hall.

KOCHMAN, T. (ed.) 1972, *Rappin' and Stylin' Out.* Chicago: University of Illinois Press.

KLEIN, W. & DITTMAR, N. 1979, *Developing Grammars*. Berlin: Springer.

KROCH, A. & SMALL, C. 1978, Grammatical ideology and its effect on speech. In D. SANKOFF (ed.), *Linguistic Variation: Models and Methods*. New York: Academic Press. pp. 45–55.

LABOV, W. 1963, The Social Motivation of a Sound Change. *Word*, 19: 273–309. Reprinted in LABOV, W. (1972), *Sociolinguistic Patterns*. Oxford: Blackwell. pp. 1–42.

— 1966, *The Social Stratification of English in New York City*. Washington, DC: Center for Applied Linguistics.

— 1969, The logic of non-standard English. *Georgetown Monographs on Language and Linguistics*, 22: 1–31. Reprinted in N. KEDDIE (ed.) (1973), *Tinker, Tailor . . . The Myth of Cultural Deprivation*. Harmondsworth, Penguin. pp. 21–66.

— 1972, *Sociolinguistic Patterns*. Oxford: Basil Blackwell.

— 1982, Objectivity and commitment in linguistic science: the case of the Black English trial in Ann Arbor. *Language in Society*, 11: 165–201.

LABOV, W., COHEN, P., ROBINS, C. & LEWIS, J. 1968, *A Study of the Non-Standard English Negro and Puerto-Rican Speakers in New York City. Report on Co-operative Research Project 3288*. New York: Columbia University.

LADO, R. 1957, *Linguistics Across Cultures*. Ann Arbor: University of Michigan Press.

LANDER, S. 1979, Morpho-syntactic features in the writing of second generation West Indians. MA dissertation, Department of English Language and Linguistics, University of Sheffield.

LAVANDERA, B. 1978, Where does the sociolinguistic variable stop? *Language in Society*, 7: 171–82.

LAWTON, D. 1980, Language Attitude, Discreteness and Code-Shifting in Jamaican Creole. *English World Wide*, 1(2): 211–26.

LEEUWENBERG, J. 1979, *Cypriots in Haringey*. Research Report No. 1, School of Librarianship. Polytechnic of North London.

LEITCH, J. 1979a, West Indian Language: the state of play. *Caribbean Teachers' Association Quarterly Newsletter*, 12.

— 1979b, West Indian language — where do we go from here? *Caribbean Teachers' Association Newsletter*, 14.

LE PAGE, R. 1957, 1958, General outlines of English Creole dialects. *Orbis*, 6: 373–91; *Orbis*, 7: 54–63.

— 1972, Preliminary report on the sociolinguistic survey of multilingual communities, part 1: Survey of Cayo District, British Honduras. *Language in Society*, 1(1): 155–72.

— 1975, "Projection, focussing and diffusion", or, steps towards a sociolinguistic theory of language. Mimeo, University of York.

LE PAGE, R. & TABOURET KELLER, A. in press, *Acts of Identity*. Cambridge: Cambridge University Press.

LINGUISTIC MINORITIES PROJECT 1984, *Linguistic Minorities in England*, Tinga Tinga.

LITTLE, R. & WILLEY, R. 1981, *Multi-Ethnic Education: The Way Forward*, Schools Council Pamphlet No. 18. London: Schools Council.

LOCAL, J., WELLS, W. & SEBBA, M. 1984, Phonetic aspects of turn delimitation in London Jamaican. *York Papers in Linguistics*, 11.

LOWENTHAL, D. 1972, *West Indian societies*. London: Oxford University Press.

MABEY, C. 1981, Black British Literacy: a study of reading attainment of London Black Children from 8 to 15 years. *Educational Research*, 23(2): 83–95.

MARKS, L. 1982, Faith in the Future. *The Observer*, December 19th: 13–14; 16.

MACAULAY, R. 1977, *Language, Social Class and Education*. Edinburgh: Edinburgh University Press.

McENTEGART, D. & LE PAGE, R. 1982, An Appraisal of the Statistical Techniques used in the Sociolinguistic Survey of Multilingual Communities. In S. ROMAINE (ed.), *Sociolinguistic Variation in Speech Communities*. London: Edward Arnold. pp. 105–24.

MACKINNON, K. 1977, *Language, Education and Social Process in a Gaelic Community*. London: Routledge and Kegan Paul.

MATARAZZO, J. 1973, A speech interaction system. In D. KEISLER (ed.), *The Process of Psychotherapy*. Chicago: Aldine.

MATTHEWS, P. 1979, *Generative Grammar and Linguistic Competence*. London: George Allen and Unwin.

MILLER, N. (ed.) 1984, *Bilingualism and Language Disability: Assessment and Remediation*. Beckenham: Croom Helm.

MILNER, D. 1983, *Children and Race: Ten Years On*. London: Ward Lock Educational.

MILROY, L. 1980, *Language and Social Networks*. Oxford: Basil Blackwell.

— 1984, What a performance! Some problems with the competence–performance distinction. *Sheffield Working Papers in Linguistics and Language*, 1: 40–55.

— forthcoming, *Observing and Analyzing Natural Language*. Oxford: Blackwell.

NATIONAL ASSOCIATION OF SCHOOLMASTERS (NAS) 1969, *Education and the Immigrants*. Hemel Hempstead, Herts: Educare.

NATALÉ, 1975, Social desirability as related to convergence of temporal speech patterns. *Perceptual and Motor Skills*, 40: 827–30.

OPEN UNIVERSITY 1982, *Minority Experience*. Milton Keynes: Open University Press.

— 1985, *Every Child's Language*. Clevedon, Avon: Multilingual Matters for the Open University.

ORTON, H. *et al.* 1962–71, *Survey of English Dialects: Basic Material*. Leeds: E. J. Arnold.

PALMER, P. 1981, An investigation into the language use of children of Jamaican origin in Manchester. MAAL project, Department of Linguistic Science, University of Reading.

PEACH, C. 1969, *West Indian Migration to Britain: a Social Geography*. Oxford: Oxford University Press.

PETRIE, P. 1972, West Indian syntax appearing in the speech of children of West Indian parentage, in the infant school. MA thesis, University of London, Institute of Education. Not available on loan.

PHILLIPS, D. 1978, Linguistic skills and ethnic group. *Research in Education*, 19: 25–37.

PLOWDEN, B. 1967, *Children and their Primary Schools*. London: HMSO.

POLLACK, M. 1972, *Today's Three Year Olds in London*. London: Heinemann.

POPLACK, S. 1980, Sometimes I'll start a sentence in English Y TERMINO EN ESPANOL: Toward a typology of code-switching. Centro Working Papers. CUNY: Centro de Estudios Puertorriquenos.

PRYCE K. 1979, *Endless Pressure*. Harmondsworth: Penguin.

PUMFREY & LEE 1982, Cultural group, reading attainments and dialect interference. *Journal of Research in Reading*, 5: 133–45.

QUIRK, R. & GREENBAUM, S. 1976, *A University Grammar of English*. London: Longman.

RAMPTON, A. 1981, *West Indian Children in Our Schools* (Interim Report of the Committee of Inquiry into the Education of Children from Ethnic Minority Groups). London: HMSO.

REISMAN, K. 1970, Cultural and Linguistic Ambiguity in a West Indian Village. In N. WHITTEN & J. SZWED (eds), *Afro-American Anthropology: Contemporary Perspectives*. New York: Free Press. pp. 129–221.

— 1974, Contrapuntal conversations in an Antiguan village. In R. BAUMAN & J. SHERZER (eds), *Explorations in the Ethnography of Speaking*. Cambridge: Cambridge University Press. pp. 110–24.

RICHMOND, J. 1979, Dialect features in mainstream school writing. *New Approaches to Multiracial Education*, 8(1): 9–15.

RICKFORD, J. 1975, Carrying the new wave into syntax: the case of Black English BIN. In R. FASOLD & R. SHUY (eds), *Analyzing Variation in Language*. Washington DC: Georgetown University Press. pp. 162–83.

ROMAINE, S. 1981, On the problem of syntactic variation: a reply to Beatriz Lavandera and William Labov, *Sociolinguistic Working Papers 82*. Austin Texas: Southwest Educational Development Laboratory. pp. 1–38.

— (ed.) 1982a, *Sociolinguistic Variation in Speech Communities*. London: Edward Arnold.

— 1982b, *Socio-historical Linguistics*. Cambridge: Cambridge University Press.

ROSEN, H. & BURGESS, T. 1980, *Languages and Dialects of London School Children*. London: Ward Lock Educational.

RUSSELL, J. 1982, Networks and sociolinguistic variation in an African suburb setting. In S. ROMAINE (ed.), *Sociolinguistic Variation in Speech Communities*. London: Edward Arnold. pp. 125–40.

RYAN, E. & CARRANZA, M. 1977, Ingroup and outgroup reactions to Mexican American language varieties. In H. GILES (ed.), *Language, Ethnicity and Intergroup Relations*. London: Academic Press. pp. 59–82.

SALKEY, A. 1969, *The Adventures of Catullus Kelly*. London: Hutchinson.

SANKOFF, G. 1980, *The Social Life of Language*. Philadelphia: University of Pennsylvania Press.

SANKOFF, G. & THIBAULT, P. 1977, L'alternance entre les auxiliaires *avoir* et *etre* en francais parle a Montreal. *Langue Francaise*, 34: 81–108.

SANKOFF, G. & VINCENT, D. 1977, L'emploi productif du *ne* dans le francais parle a Montreal. *Le Francais Moderne*, 45: 243–56.

SCARMAN, LORD 1981, *The Brixton Disorders, 10–12 April, 1981*. London: HMSO.

SCHOOLS COUNCIL 1972, *Teaching English to West Indian Children, Concept 7–9*. London: Edward Arnold.

SCOTTON, C. 1980, Explaining linguistic choices as identity negotiations. In H. GILES, P. ROBINSON & P. SMITH (eds), *Language: Social Psychological Perspectives*. Oxford: Pergamon. pp. 359–66.

SEBBA, M. 1984a, Serial Verb or Syntactic Calque: the Great Circuit of *say*. Paper presented at the 5th Biennial Meeting of the Society for Caribbean Linguistics.

— 1984b, Language Change among Afro-Caribbeans in London. *Amsterdam Creole Studies*, 7: 1–11.

— 1984c, Fluent and non-fluent speakers of London Jamaican: observations on the concepts of "native speaker" and "mother tongue speaker". Paper presented at the conference on Languages without a Written Tradition and their Role in Education.

— in press, London Jamaican and Black London English. In D. SUTCLIFFE & A. WONG (eds), *Language and the British Black Experience*. Oxford: Blackwell.

SEBBA, M. & LE PAGE, R. 1983, Transplanted parents, indigenous children: the linguistic symptoms of fresh cultural groupings. Paper presented at the Society for Caribbean Linguistics Annual Meeting.

SEBBA, M. & WHITE, F. forthcoming, The role of Creole in mother tongue education. London: National Council for Mother Tongue Teaching.

SEBBA, M. & WOOTTON, T. 1984, Conversational code-switching in London Jamaican. Paper presented to Sociolinguistics Symposium 5, Liverpool.

SELINKER, L. 1972, Interlanguage. (*International Review of Applied Linguistics*, 10(3): 219–31). Reprinted in J. RICHARDS (ed.), *Error Analysis*. London: Longman. pp. 31–54.

SELVON, S. 1972, *The Lonely Londoners*. Harlow: Longman.

SHUY, R., WOLFRAM, W. & RILEY, W. 1968, *Field Techniques in Urban Language Study*. Washington DC: Center for Applied Linguistics.

SINGH, R. 1979, *Sikhs in Bradford*. Bradford College.

SMITH, D. 1976, *The Facts of Racial Disadvantage*. London: Political and Economic Planning.

SMITH, F. 1978, *Reading*. Cambridge: Cambridge University Press.

SMITH, G. 1984, *Sampling Linguistic Minorities: a Technical Report on the Adult Language use Survey*. Linguistic Minorities Project Working Paper No. 4, University of London Institute of Education.

SMITHERMAN, G. 1981, *Talkin' and Testifyin'*. Boston: Houghton Mifflin.

SMOLINS, G. 1974, Reading and comprehension: a comparative study of some 8–9 year old children of English and West Indian origin. MA dissertation, Department of Applied Linguistics, Birkbeck College, University of London.

SNEDECOR, G. & COCHRAN, W. 1967, *Statistical Methods*. 3rd edition. Ames, Iowa: Iowa State University Press.

SPENDER, D. 1980, *Man Made Language*. London: Routledge and Kegan Paul.

STONE, M. 1981, The Education of the Black Child in Britain: the Myth of Multiracial Education. London: Fontana.

STUBBS, M. & HILLIER, H. 1983, *Readings on Language, Schools and Classrooms*. London: Methuen.

SUTCLIFFE, D. 1976, Hou dem taak in Bedford, Sa. *Multiracial School*, 5: 19–24.

— 1978, The Language of First and Second Generation West Indian Children in Bedfordshire. M.Ed thesis, University of Leicester.

— 1982a, *British Black English*. Oxford: Basil Blackwell.

— 1982b, British Black Narrative Patterns. Report to the ESRC.

— 1982c, Verbal patterns and syntactic tone in Jamaican Creole 1. Paper given at the Fourth Biennial Conference of the Society for Caribbean Linguistics, Paramaribo, Suriname.

— forthcoming, *Language Symbolism*. Clevedon, Avon: Multilingual Matters.

SUTCLIFFE, D. & TOMLIN, C. in press, The Black Churches. In D. SUTCLIFFE & A. WONG (eds), *Language and the British Black experience*. Oxford: Blackwell.

SUTCLIFFE, D. & WONG, A. (eds) in press, *Language and the British Black Experience*. Oxford: Blackwell.

TALK WORKSHOP GROUP 1982, *Becoming Our Own Experts. The Vauxhall Papers*. Available from the ILEA English Centre, Sutherland Street, London SW1.

TAJFEL, H. 1974, Social identity and intergroup behaviour. *Social Science Information*, 13, 65–93.

— (ed.) 1977, *Differentiation Between Social Groups: Studies in the Social Psychology of Intergroup Relations*. London: Academic Press.

— (ed.) 1978, *Differentiation between Social Groups: Studies in the Social Psychology of Intergroup Relations*. London: Academic Press.

— 1982, The social psychology of minorities. In C. HUSBAND (ed.), *"Race" in Britain: Continuity and Change*. London: Hutchinson. pp. 216–58.

TAJFEL, H. & TURNER, J. 1979, An integrative theory of intergroup conflict. In W. AUSTIN & H. WORCHEL (eds), *The Social Psychology of Intergroup Relations*. Monterey: Brooks-Cole. pp. 33–53.

TAYLOR, D. 1980, Ethnicity and language: a social psychological perspective. In H. GILES, P. ROBINSON & P. SMITH (eds), *Language: Social Psychological Perspectives*. Oxford: Pergamon. pp. 133–39.

TEITELBAUM, H. 1979, Unreliability of language background self-ratings for young bilingual children. *Child Study Journal*, 9: 51–9.

THOMAS, R. 1979, Vindication and infringement towards an ethnographic analysis of classroom interaction. MA dissertation, University of London Institute of Education. Not available on loan.

THORNE, B. & HENLEY N. (eds) 1975, *Language and Sex: Difference and Dominance*. Rowley, Mass: Newbury House.

TIZARD, B. & HUGHES, M. 1984, *Young Children Learning*. London: Fontana.

TODD, L. 1974, *Pidgins and Creoles*. London: Routledge and Kegan Paul.

TOMLIN, C. 1981, The extent to which West Indian language differences hinder or enhance learning. Unpublished dissertation, Dudley College of Education.

TOMLINSON, S. 1980, Ethnic minority parents and education. In M. CRAFT, J. RAYNOR & L. COHEN (eds), *Linking Home and School*. 3rd Edition. London: Harper and Row.

— 1984, *Home and School in Multicultural Britain*. London: Batsford.

TOWNSEND, H. 1971, *Immigrants in England: the LEA response*. Windsor: National Foundation for Educational Research.

TROIKE, R. 1969, Receptive competence, productive competence and performance. *Georgetown Round Table Meeting on Linguistics and Language Studies*, 20: 63–69.

TROYNA, B. 1979, Differential commitment to ethnic identity by black youths in Britain, *New Community*, 7: 406–14.

TROYNA, B. & SMITH, D. I. (eds) 1983, *Racism, School and the Labour Market*. Leicester: National Youth Bureau.

TRUDGILL, P. 1974, *The Social Differentiation of English in Norwich*. Cambridge: Cambridge University Press.

— (ed.) 1978, *Sociolinguistic Patterns in British English*. London: Edward Arnold.

— (ed.) 1984, *Language in the British Isles*. Cambridge: Cambridge University Press.

URE, J. 1974, Code-switching and "mixed speech" in the register systems of developing languages. In A. VERDOOT (ed.), *Proceedings of the 3rd International Congress of Applied Linguistics*. Vol. 11: *Applied Sociolinguistics*. Heidelberg: Julius Groos Verlag.

WALVIN, J. 1982, Black caricature: the roots of racialism. In C. HUSBAND (ed.), *"Race" in Britain: Continuity and Change*. London: Hutchinson.

WELLS, J. 1973, *Jamaican Pronunciation in London*. Publications of the Philological Society. Oxford: Blackwell.

— 1982, *Accents of English: Beyond the British Isles*. Cambridge: Cambridge University Press.

WEINREICH, U. 1968, *Languages in Contact*. The Hague: Mouton.
WHITEMAN, M., BROWN, B. & DEUTSCH, M. 1967, Some effects of social class and race on children's language and intellectual abilities. In M. DEUTSCH (ed.), *The Disadvantaged Child*. New York: Basic Books.
WHITTEN, N. & SZWED, J. (eds) 1970, *Afro-American Anthropology: Contemporary Perspectives*. New York: Free Press.
WIGHT, J. 1969, Teaching English to West Indian Children. *English for Immigrants* 2(2) and ATEPO (1970). *Work Group on West Indian Report*. pp. 58–60.
— 1970, Language Deprivation and Remedial Teaching Techniques, in ATEPO. *Work Group on West Indian Pupils Report*.
— 1971, Dialect in school. *Educational Review*, 24(1): 47–58.
— 1976, How much interference? *Times Educational Supplement*, 14 May.
WIGHT, J. & NORRIS, R. 1970, *Teaching English to West Indian Children: the Research Stage of the Project*. Schools Council Working Paper 29. London: Evans/Methuen Educational.
WILSON, D. 1978, Rationale for a West Indian language course for primary schools. *Torch Special Issue*, 3. Kingston, Jamaica: Ministry of Education.
WILSON, D., CRAIG, D. & CAMPBELL, H. 1979, *Teacher's Book, Year 1, Term 1*. Kingston: Jamaica: Heinemann Educational Books.
WINFORD, D. 1972, A sociolinguistic description of two communities in Trinidad. Ph.D thesis, University of York.
— 1984, The linguistic variable and syntactic variation in creole continua. *Lingua*, 62: 267–88.
WOLFSON, N. 1976, Speech events and natural speech: some implications for sociolinguistic methodology. *Language in Society*, 5: 189–209.
WOOD, C. 1974, Life styles among West Indians and social work problems. *New Community*, 3(3): 249–54.
WRIGHT, F. 1984, A Sociolinguistic Study of Passivization among Black Adolescents in Britain. Unpublished Ph.D thesis, University of Birmingham.
YOUNG, C. 1973, Belize Creole: a Study of the Creolized English Spopken in the City of Belize in its Cultural and Social Setting. Unpublished D.Phil thesis, University of York.
YOUNG, M. & WILMOTT, P. 1962, *Family and Kinship in East London*. Harmondsworth: Penguin.

Index